# Distilling Chinese Education into 8 Concepts

# Other Books by the Author

*Teacher Tenure: An Analysis of the Critical Elements* (2015)
*An Instructor Primer for Adjunct and New Faculty: Foundations for Career Success* (2013)
*High-Poverty, High-Performing Schools: Foundations for Real Student Success* (2011)
*Equalize Student Achievement: Prioritizing Money and Power* (2010)
*Pivotal Strategies for the Educational Leader: The Importance of Sun Tzu's Art of War* (2007)
*Using Data Analysis to Improve Student Learning: Toward 100% Proficiency* (2006)

# Distilling Chinese Education into 8 Concepts

Ovid K. Wong

ROWMAN & LITTLEFIELD
Lanham • Boulder • New York • London

Published by Rowman & Littlefield
A wholly owned subsidiary of The Rowman & Littlefield Publishing Group, Inc.
4501 Forbes Boulevard, Suite 200, Lanham, Maryland 20706
www.rowman.com

Unit A, Whitacre Mews, 26-34 Stannary Street, London SE11 4AB

Copyright © 2017 by Ovid K. Wong

*All rights reserved.* No part of this book may be reproduced in any form or by any electronic or mechanical means, including information storage and retrieval systems, without written permission from the publisher, except by a reviewer who may quote passages in a review.

British Library Cataloguing in Publication Information Available

Library of Congress Cataloging-in-Publication Data Available

ISBN 978-1-4758-2193-2 (cloth : alk. paper)
ISBN 978-1-4758-2194-9 (pbk : alk. paper)
ISBN 978-1-4758-2195-6 (electronic)

∞ ™ The paper used in this publication meets the minimum requirements of American National Standard for Information Sciences Permanence of Paper for Printed Library Materials, ANSI/NISO Z39.48-1992.

Printed in the United States of America

This book is dedicated to two young sprouts, Jayden and Mia, who do not yet know about the Chinese way of education, based on a long-running intellectual foundation. It is hoped that they will appreciate the value of good education when they grow up to become big and strong trees.

# Contents

| | | |
|---|---|---|
| List of Figures | | ix |
| Foreword | | xi |
| Introduction | | xiii |
| 1 | Success | 1 |
| 2 | Meritocracy | 13 |
| 3 | Parents | 27 |
| 4 | Schooling | 37 |
| 5 | Cram Schools | 59 |
| 6 | Examinations | 73 |
| 7 | Face | 89 |
| 8 | Connections | 101 |
| Afterword | | 113 |
| Appendix: A Chronology of China | | 115 |
| References | | 117 |
| About the Author | | 119 |

# List of Figures

| | | |
|---|---|---|
| Fig. 1.1 | Chinese characters for success. | 5 |
| Fig. 1.2 | Chinese slogan banner. | 6 |
| Fig. 1.3 | Meritocracy. | 11 |
| Fig. 2.1 | Education as societal equalizer. | 17 |
| Fig. 2.2 | Education as societal sorter. | 20 |
| Fig. 2.3 | 2015 weekly earnings by educational attainment. | 22 |
| Fig. 2.4 | 2015 unemployment rates by educational attainment. | 23 |
| Fig. 2.5 | Anshun University student ranking. | 24 |
| Fig. 4.1 | Educational system in China. | 46 |
| Fig. 4.2 | Study habits. | 49 |
| Fig. 4.3 | Morning reading. | 50 |
| Fig. 4.4 | Teacher-centered curriculum. | 51 |
| Fig. 4.5 | Student-centered curriculum. | 53 |
| Fig. 4.6 | Typical school day in China. | 56 |
| Fig. 5.1 | Cram school small-group activity. | 62 |
| Fig. 5.2 | Tutor kings and queens. | 67 |
| Fig. 6.1 | The *gaokao* structure. | 78 |

| | | |
|---|---|---|
| Fig. 6.2 | Subject selection for *gaokao*. | 80 |
| Fig. 6.3 | Mathematics sample question 1. | 81 |
| Fig. 6.4 | Mathematics sample question 2. | 81 |
| Fig. 6.5 | Study abroad advertisement. | 85 |
| Fig. 7.1 | The yin and yang of face. | 94 |
| Fig. 8.1 | Connections. | 104 |
| Fig. 8.2 | Elements of relationships. | 112 |

# Foreword

China is well known to the world for its five thousand years of civilization. And yet this ancient nation and the Chinese mind-set are a mystery to many. When we observe one's behavior, we are not just looking at the surface; we need to dig deeper and learn about the culture and backdrop behind it. How can we explain the complexity of the Chinese civilization that spans from ancient to modern times?

We are privileged to have Dr. Ovid Wong, who, as a renowned educator and a knowledgeable scholar, can master both the cultures from the West and the East. I am delighted to invite people to read this book, *Distilling Chinese Education into 8 Concepts*. Since Dr. Wong is an expert in the field of education, he is confident in explaining the differences between the educational systems in the Western world (particularly in the United States) and China. He uses his expertise to illustrate the Chinese culture through the aspect of education. He innovatively thought of eight conceptual words to "distill" education in China.

In this book, you will find many interesting Chinese idioms, such as "Men cannot live without a face and trees cannot live without bark" and "Kill the chicken to scare the monkey," to name just two. More importantly, one can also learn about the forces in China that drive the competitiveness of Chinese education today. Dr. Wong pairs his thorough explanation of these eight concepts with lots of real-life examples, illustrations, and fact-based analysis. As a result, one can better understand why modern Chinese people behave the way they do today. I encourage you to consider the following questions:

1. What is the meaning of *success* in a Chinese person's mind?
2. How does the educational system function as an "equalizer for all social classes" in the Western world, whereas it functions as a "societal sorter" in China?
3. How do Chinese parents involve themselves in their children's education as compared to Western parents?
4. What is convergent and divergent thinking in Chinese education?
5. How does the "ultimate cram school" in China compare to the prep centers in the United States?
6. What is China's "fifth big invention," after the compass, the printing press, paper, and gunpowder?
7. What are the nine popular Chinese expressions about Chinese "face culture"?
8. What are the etiquettes of impressions and connections in human relationships?

You will find yourself richly blessed with fascinating information from reading Dr. Wong's well-thought-out book.

Rev. James Ip
vice president and associate professor of the Old Testament
Christian Witness Theological Seminary

# Introduction

As a proud graduate of the University of Illinois at Urbana-Champaign (UIUC), decades ago I had the opportunity to revisit the university for a professional conference. At that time, a number of new academic buildings had arisen on the campus, and it was obvious that the university had grown. To my surprise the college town of Urbana-Champaign looked different not only because of the new buildings but also because of the great change in student diversity.

One can see crowds of international students, particularly many Chinese, on campus. While enjoying my lunch at the ever-popular student union building cafeteria, for a split moment I thought I was on campus somewhere in China! Students at the lunch table even joked around, referring to UIUC as the University of China in Illinois. Do you know that UIUC has one of the highest Chinese student enrollments in the United States?

UIUC is not the only university in the United States where Chinese students make up over 10 percent of the total undergraduate and graduate enrollment. Michigan State University is not far behind, followed by Purdue University Indianapolis and the University of Southern California (USC). Students at the latter have even nicknamed it the University of So-many Chinese.

In the past, Chinese students in the United States were mostly graduate students living on shoestring budgets. That is not true anymore; now a large number are from China's wealthy and elite families. Some well-heeled parents even send their kids away to college with a generous endowment of real estate and luxury cars. Do you know that the daughter of President Xi Jinping studied at Harvard under another name? It is believed that President Xi himself admires Western culture and education.

Businesses in big cities have capitalized on the new buying power of Chinese students. Bergdorf Goodman, the New York City–based department store, sponsored Chinese New Year celebrations at New York University and Columbia, and a fashion show was organized for Chinese students at the Bloomingdale's shopping center in Chicago. Dealing with Chinese students is quickly becoming a profitable business in the United States.

The number of Chinese students attending private American high schools has also been growing for more than a decade, according to the Department of Homeland Security's Student and Exchange Visitor Program. Well-off Chinese parents want to avoid the pressure-cooker educational system at home and give their children a better chance of academic success in the United States.

How can one possibly miss the prominent advertisements at the Beijing airport inviting parents to bring their school-age children to the United States for various experiences, such as summer sports camps and college tours? Travel agencies offer other US educational tours for high school students to develop their academic and leadership potential.

Can you imagine reading another sports magazine article aboard a Chinese domestic flight and seeing an advertisement saying that experience matters in the travel adventure? The ad suggests visiting Boston, the education capital of the United States, and indulging in the Harvard and MIT experience. Are you still not convinced that the United States remains the top educational choice for students from China?

American people in general view the influx of students into the US educational system in two opposing ways: as Sinophiles or Sinophobes. Sinophilia, or a love of China, is positive because the fresh supply of full-paying students for the educational system translates into a multi-billion-dollar import business every year. The student import is different from the affordable "Made in China" merchandise at Walmart and other department stores because Chinese students bring in cash and bolster shrinking enrollment and the dwindling economy.

Other examples of educational Sinophilia include a bill calling for the United States to spend $1.3 billion over five years on a Chinese-language program in 2004; the implementation of a Chinese-language immersion program developed jointly by the University of Oregon and Portland Public Schools in 2005; the offering of an Advanced Placement test in Chinese, commonly known as AP Chinese, in 2007; and more recently the administration of "Chinese Connect" in Chicago, the largest public school Chinese program in the nation. Believe it or not, Chinese is the most widely spoken first language in the world due to the sheer size of the country's population.

Sinophobia, or fear of China, on the other hand, is less positive and arises because the large number of students from the far side of the globe enhances school diversity but dilutes the traditional American school character. To ensure that immigrant students are academically successful, new service programs are added, appropriate instructional methods are developed, and curricula are modified to meet the new school requirements.

At the college level, the use of racial classifications in admissions is criticized. Prestigious institutions of higher education like Harvard and the University of California at Berkeley have been accused of holding Chinese Americans to a higher standard of admission, violating their civil rights. Studies show that Chinese Americans have better academic standing than members of other ethnic groups but are disproportionately rejected for admission. Does this reflect other student groups' fear of being displaced by the overwhelming number of academically qualified and overqualified Chinese students?

Many educators are pulling their hair out because they do not understand how to work well with new Chinese immigrant students and their parents. To get the job done, one must go beyond the superficial language barrier to understanding the culture that shapes the base foundations of learning and thinking. Some people ask whether the new wave of student immigration might challenge the effectiveness of the school systems. Or is it more honest to ask whether the question is just another manifestation of xenophobia?

The perennial wisdom of Sun Tzu, a very prominent Chinese military strategist and philosopher, is pertinent to understanding this book's conception. In his well-read *The Art of War*, Sun Tzu writes, "Know yourself [i.e., the educators] and know your enemy [i.e., students] and you will win in every battle." Please understand that the word *enemy* here is used as an analogy. The purpose of this book is not to further weigh the pros and cons of immigrant Chinese students in the United States or US students going abroad to study in China. It seeks to better illustrate the intricate elements of Chinese education compared to American education and thereby help educators and policy-makers to craft win-win decisions in the education encounter of the dragon and the eagle.

China's more than five-thousand-year history predates the advent three thousand years ago of graphical recording of events. How has education in China developed to become what it is today?

The task of selecting inclusive conceptual words while researching the book in China was difficult. There is so much information that the number of possible words exceeded ten. Magically a number came to mind through a merger of small ideas into big concepts. The Chinese pronunciation of the number 8, *ba*, sounds like the pronunciation of *fa*, which means "prosperity" and "success." Welcome to *Distilling Chinese Education into 8 Concepts*!

*Chapter One*

# Success

"A year's harvest counts on spring; a man's success counts on diligence."

### THE FIRESIDE CHAT

Soon after the last day of the winter final examination, a group of international Chinese students came together to modestly celebrate the completion of their most recent college semester in the United States. This student support group holds scheduled meetings, allowing them to share their aspirations and challenges and to support each other. The small group likes to meet at the fireside lounge of the ever-popular student union building because it is conveniently located on campus and is usually quiet, with comfortable sofas. Regular members of this group are Katy Wang, Shan-Shan Zhang, Li-Fan Long, Yen-Chi Liang, Sun-Yu Chi, Fei-Fei Tian, Douglas Chen, and Chung-Wai Gong.

Katy Wang comes from Beijing, the capital city of China. Her family believes that she needs to take charge of her own destiny through diligent work—schoolwork. Academically, she was an average student in China and could not get into a top-tier local university. Her aspiration to succeed prompted her to venture overseas to the United States through the support of her family and her own savings. Katy is in America training to become a certified accountant and has a promising career. She says, "I learn how to invest and how to manage resources. I want to be a successful businesswoman."

Shan-Shan Zhang believes that a sure way to make it in the world is to take charge in life. She came from Dalian, a beautiful coastal seaport city in northeastern China. She believes strongly that she can get ahead as long as she applies herself in life. To her pleasant surprise, she received a modest scholarship to study at the university. The scholarship is more important to her as recognition of her good work than as a source of free money. Shan-Shan is a business major at the university and hopes to make it in the world as a reputable investor at a major US bank after graduation. "My computation skills are noted as compared to my other American classmates. On the other hand, I wish I can speak and write like my American friends. At the end of my training, I know that I need both my subject-matter expertise and communication skills," says Shan-Shan.

Li-Fan Long came to the United States as a bright graduate student from Shenyang, the capital city of Liaoning, in northeastern China. He is very good in mathematics and computers and was a wiz junior computer programmer in China. He believes that adding an advanced degree in project management will help him to expand his father's tech business in China. Li-Fan is a research assistant at the university and often helps his classmates with their computer homework. He says, "I am good in math and computers, and this will be my passport to a good career when I graduate. I share what I know about computer science, and in return my American friends teach me English; we help each other out in schoolwork."

Yen-Chi Liang is a chemical engineering major. His best high school subjects were chemistry and mathematics. He came to the United States from Hong Kong years after the former British colony reverted to China in 1997. Much of his thinking is evidence-based and logical, and this can be connected to his foundational training in science and mathematics. "I would consider myself successful when I gain fame and material possession, and is this not logical? Look at Michelle Wu. She is a Harvard Law School graduate paving her way to become the first Asian American woman to be the Boston City Council President!" Yen-Chi applied to several US graduate programs and was lucky enough to get accepted by all of them. He decided to attend a prestigious institution, believing that a degree from a high-ranking university would help him land a well-paid job down the road, possibly in government.

Sun-Yu Chi comes from a good family, and his parents tell him that his top priority in life is to graduate from a good college. He came to the United States because he could not get into a top college in Shanghai, China. He did not give up, however, and followed the advice of his parents to further his education in the United States after high school. "Success is doing well in school and finding a good job when you are done; it could be that simple," says Sun-Yu optimistically. "The one challenge facing me is the embarrassment of sharing my ideas in class. I hesitate to share when I am unsure whether my ideas are good or even valid. The expectation of expressing my ideas fluently in English is often a scary experience."

Fei-Fei Tian is a controlling person, and his confidence stems from being a top student from ZhongShan High School in China. He is currently also a top student in his college class in the United States. It is no surprise that Fei-Fei is such a strong and self-reliant person. He says, "I believe that I am the only person who can help me because of my good school grades, and other people around me (except my parents and professors) do not matter much. With my father's connections, I would like to go back to China after graduation and secure a government job."

Douglas Chen, from a family in Guangzhou, China, believes strongly in academic success and being the master of his own destiny. As a student, he sailed smoothly through the rigorous Chinese public examination system. He was accepted at a state-run university in China and decided instead to broaden his academic horizons in the United States, following his uncle's footsteps. His family is well-to-do and elite in Guangzhou, so paying full college tuition in the United States is the least of their problems. Douglas says, "Doing well in college should not be a problem because my field of interest is science and technology and the achievement as such does not depend so much on the mastery of the English language. My plan is to return to Guangzhou after graduation here because I need to help and expand my parents' food-manufacturing business."

Chung-Wai Gong comes from a small village in Fuzhou, China. He is the only child in the family. As a youngster, he dreamed of going to college, getting a lucrative job, and eventually securing a good future. Chung-Wai is a food science major, and this is his second-to-last semester at the university. When asked about finding a job after graduation, he says, "My chance of getting a job here in America is better than in China because I am good in my field and the employment competition here is less keen. I want to go back to China after a few years of work; I feel obligated to attend to the needs of my aging parents back in Fuzhou."

One can say that these Chinese students have much in common in terms of their backgrounds and motivation to excel. They differ little from students from other countries like the United States. With no exceptions, they all want to pursue better lives and prosperity. It is clear from the fireside chat that key to realizing their dreams are both family and education. In the minds of these ambitious young students, the dream has the potential to reel in personal fame and eventually to honor the family. In that sense, the prosperity concept goes beyond the individualism of the student to collectivism of the family.

## THE PERCEPTION OF SUCCESS

The students at the fireside chat raised the idea of life's success, and the two Chinese characters for success (figure 1.1) well represent its nature in the context of Chinese education. The two characters read from left to right as *cheng gong*. The words stem historically from radicals of the Chinese written language in the form of a picture or just the meaning. Written Chinese language is complex, and it is classified by the radicals of the character.

Compare the following two Chinese characters: 採 and 踩. The two words have the same right-hand radical. To find the meaning, one needs to analyze the left-hand radical. One is 扌, and the other is 足. The 扌 radical means "hand," so one can guess that it is a word related to the hand. The 足 radical means "foot," and one can guess that it is a word related to the foot. 採 is a verb, and it means to "pick with the hand." 踩 is also a verb, and it means to "stomp with the foot." Such is the magic of using the radical to extract the meaning of Chinese characters.

Let us now go back to the two characters for success. The left-hand character, 成, has the radical for "spear"; it is an ancient Chinese weapon. What, then, is the relevance of a spear in success? The connection is competition. In the ancient Chinese world, warriors used weapons of sorts to compete for victory. One can induce from the spear radical that competition is a component for attaining success, and in chapter 6 you will see the fierce nature of academic competition in Chinese education.

The right-hand character 功 has two radicals for "task" and "effort," respectively. Here, the "effort" radical refers to strength. The two characters *cheng gong*, or *success*, in Chinese are powerful in meaning and have been used commonly in names. Zheng Cheng Gong (1624–1662, see appendix) is someone with success as part of his name. He defeated the Dutch pirates to recover the island of Taiwan for the motherland. He is a famous folk hero of China.

A group of characters that make up phrases with a certain meaning are idioms. These develop from popular social usage, and some have a story.

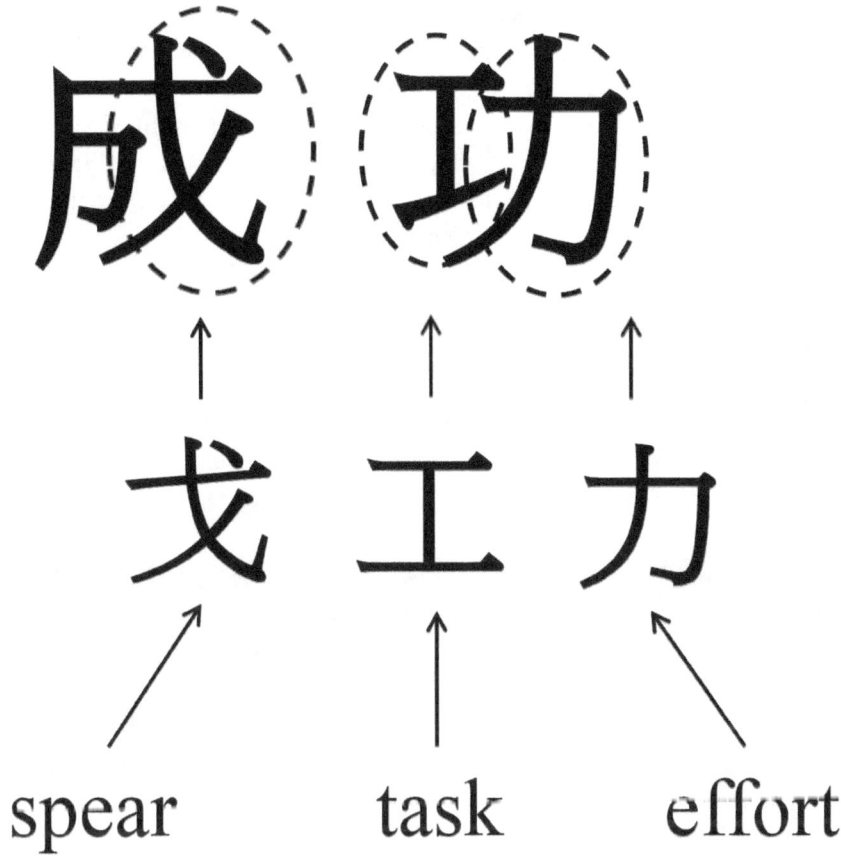

**Figure 1.1. Chinese characters for success.**

Many idioms are literary in meaning, and the story can be traced from some written historic source. Others originate from all walks of life and from past generations.

An attribute of a Chinese idiom is an equal number of characters in each segment. Figure 1.2 shows a banner slogan evolved from an idiom format that has two segments, as seen in the two vertical banners on display on campus at Dalian Nationalities University. The slogan takes the structure of an idiom. The right banner reads, "Focus teaching, emphasize learning." The left banner reads, "Respect teacher, love students." The first segment has four characters and is balanced by the second segment, which also has four characters.

The slogan describes the noble quality of education and the professional relationship between the teachers and students. It is a reminder that education is not only a theory but also a practice that takes place in the real classroom. Amusingly, the educational ideal of respect and diligence sometimes contrasts with what we see in public school classrooms in the United States.

"A year's harvest counts on spring; a man's success counts on diligence" is a Chinese idiom quoted at the beginning of the chapter. In traditional Chinese agrarian society, farmers plan their harvests by sowing seeds during the growing season of spring and working hard throughout the year to care for the crops. The proverb refers to the qualities of wisdom in planning and diligence in attaining success. People who are not farmers do not have to deal with agricultural work; nevertheless, planning and diligence still apply.

Do you know why China was successful in the 2008 Olympics? Chinese athletes are trained to believe that hard work gets results. These athletes

**Figure 1.2. Chinese slogan banner.**

practice year-round. Thus, having followed a long period of training, they optimized their efforts to win the medals.

Please remember that, for many Chinese scholars, success means not just getting the job done but getting the job done well. Does this not reinforce the competitive nature of success in Chinese education?

When put together, the two Chinese characters for success carry the ingredients of competition and human effort to achieve success! At this time, one might be curious about the role of intelligence in attaining success. That curiosity can be addressed by the Confucian culture of diligence over intelligence to mean that, by working hard enough, a person can compensate for his shortcomings in mental abilities. A smart student may finish his homework in a half hour; the slow student may spend more time to get the job done. What matters is that both students complete their homework regardless of the time spent. The impact of Confucian culture on Chinese education is deep and will be discussed throughout the book.

*Success* is hard to define because different people have different views of its meaning. For example, to a student, success is getting a good education; to an established business person, it is expanding the business and opening subsidiaries. Listening closely to the fireside chat, one can interpret what success is to these Chinese students:

- I want to be a successful businesswoman.
- I wish to apply myself in life.
- I am good in math and computers, and this will be my passport to a good career when I graduate.
- I would consider myself successful when I gain fame and material possession, and is this not logical?
- A degree from a high-ranking university will help to land a well-paid job down the road, possibly in government.
- My top priority in life is to graduate from a good college.
- I would like to go back to China after graduation and secure a government job.
- My plan is to return to Guangzhou after graduation here because I need to help and expand my parents' food-manufacturing business.
- I hope to get a lucrative job and eventually secure a good future.

*Chapter 1*

# FROM A HUNAN VILLAGE TO THE HARVARD COMMENCEMENT PODIUM

In 2016, He Jiang made history by being the first Chinese national PhD recipient in biochemistry ever to speak from behind the Harvard commencement podium. He came from a humble beginning in a small farming village in Hunan, China. His parents never even graduated from high school. He worked extremely hard and achieved meritorious academic recognition first from the top-ranked Anhui University of Science and Technology in China with a full scholarship, and he continued his graduate study at Harvard, also with a scholarship.

The academic success of He Jiang is something that many Chinese scholars can only envy because Harvard is the Holy Grail of the academic quest. Ask students what work they wish to do when they grow up, and many will pick a profession that requires rigorous training, such as scientist or engineer. Ask students what college they dream of attending, and many will say Harvard; some might not even know where Harvard is located. He Jiang has achieved both because he is a biochemist with a PhD from Harvard. He is the new student role model, and many will follow his footsteps to academic success.

He was picked from among thousands to speak on behalf of his fellow graduates. What follows is his original commencement speech in English, given at Harvard University in 2016:

> When I was in middle school, a poisonous spider bit my right hand. I ran to my mom for help—but instead of taking me to the doctor, my mom set my hand on fire.
>
> After wrapping my hand with several layers of cotton, then soaking it in wine, she put a chopstick in my mouth, and ignited the cotton. Heat quickly penetrated the cotton and began to roast my hand. The searing pain made me want to scream, but the chopstick prevented it. All I could do was watch my hand burn—one minute, then two minutes—until mom put out the fire.
>
> You see, the part of China I grew up in was a rural village, and at that time pre-industrial. When I was born, my village had no cars, no telephones, no electricity, not even running water. And we certainly didn't have access to modern medical resources. There was no doctor my mother could bring me to see about my spider bite.
>
> For those who study biology, you may have grasped the science behind my mom's cure: heat deactivates proteins, and a spider's venom is simply a form of protein. It's cool how that folk remedy incorporates basic biochemistry,

isn't it? But I am a PhD student in biochemistry at Harvard. I now know better, less painful and less risky treatments existed. So I can't help but ask myself, why I didn't receive one at the time?

Fifteen years have passed since that incident. I am happy to report that my hand is fine. But the question lingers, and I continue to be troubled by the unequal distribution of scientific knowledge throughout the world. We have learned to edit the human genome and unlock many secrets of how cancer progresses. We can manipulate neuronal activity literally with the switch of a light. Each year brings more advances in biomedical research—exciting, transformative accomplishments. Yet, despite the knowledge we have amassed, we haven't been so successful in deploying it to where it is needed most. According to the World Bank, twelve percent of the world's population lives on less than $2 a day. Malnutrition kills more than 3 million children annually. Three hundred million people are afflicted by malaria globally. All over the world, we constantly see these problems of poverty, illness, and lack of resources impeding the flow of scientific information. Lifesaving knowledge we take for granted in the modern world is often unavailable in these underdeveloped regions. And in far too many places, people are still essentially trying to cure a spider bite with fire.

While studying at Harvard, I saw how scientific knowledge can help others in simple, yet profound ways. The bird flu pandemic in the 2000s looked to my village like a spell cast by demons. Our folk medicine didn't even have half-measures to offer. What's more, farmers didn't know the difference between common cold and flu; they didn't understand that the flu is much more lethal than the common cold. Most people were also unaware that the virus could transmit across different species.

So when I realized the simple hygiene practices like separating different animal species could contain the spread of the disease, and that I could make the knowledge available to my village, that was my first "aha" moment as a budding scientist. But it was more than that; it was a vital inflection point in my ethical development, my own self-understanding as a member of the global community.

Harvard dares us to dream big, to aspire to change the world. Here on this Commencement Day, we are probably thinking of grand destinations and big adventures that await us. As for me, I am also thinking of the farmers in my village. My experience here reminds me of how important it is for researchers to communicate our knowledge to those who need it. Because my using the science that we already have, we could probably bring my village and thousands like it into the world you and I take for granted every day. And that's an impact every one of us can make!

But the question is, will we make the effort or not?

More than ever before, our society emphasizes science and innovation. But an equally important emphasis should be on distributing the knowledge we have to where it's needed. Changing the world does not mean that everyone has to find the next big thing. It can be as simple as becoming a better communicator, and finding more creative ways to pass on the knowledge we have to people like my mom and farmers in their local community. Our society also needs to recognize that the equal distribution of knowledge is a pivotal step to human development, and work to bring this into reality.

And if we do that, then perhaps a teenager in rural China who is bitten by a spider will not have to burn his hand, but will know to seek a doctor instead.

## THE SHADOW BEHIND SUCCESS

It is unfair to draw any conceptual generalizations from the academic success of Harvard scholar He Jiang and students from the fireside chat; nevertheless, in the mind of many common Chinese people, wealth and power remain the significant symbols of success. The lucky number for Chinese is eight. Why? The pronunciation of *eight*, or *ba*, is similar to the pronunciation of *fa*, which means "to make a lot of money." Obsession over *fa* is expressed sumptuously by Chinese in license plate numbers, telephone numbers, passwords, or other numerical representations. One other expression of wealth in a number combination is 168. The meaning of *eight* has already been explained, but how about *one* and *six*? The Chinese pronunciation of *one* and *six* in the southern regional dialect sounds like "all the way." Now when *one*, *six*, and *eight* get strung together, it sounds like "making money all the way." Are you still unconvinced that wealth is an integral element of success in the Chinese culture?

A path to wealth and power may regrettably lead a person to the dark side of greed and corruption. But in the context of He Jiang's commencement message, knowledge, which is a form of wealth, and the ability to share that wealth will eventually make the world a better place. Success not properly attained should not be held. However, wealth and power earned through moving up the bureaucracy honestly is never regarded as improper. So what is new in ethics?

Unique to the Chinese are the critical elements people encounter through the paths that lead them to success. We are sure that He Jiang, the Harvard scholar, had already jumped a lot of hurdles before reaching his academic goals. When success in life (figure 1.3) is mapped backward, one can identify seven elements, which are the illusive intangibles that form the shadow behind the ultimate life's goal:

1. Meritocracy (merit-based competition)
2. Family aspiration and support
3. Purposeful school education
4. Supportive after-school activities
5. High-stakes public examinations
6. The pervasive culture of face, or *mianzi*
7. The pervasive culture of connections, or *guanxi*

In figure 1.3, the seven elements plus success yield the ultimate eight concepts about education in China. In the center of the big picture is the overarching concept of meritocracy, a system valued by the Chinese to compete and be the best they can be to achieve success (chapter 2). On the left of the figure is a group of three concepts, with parents topping the list. The family is an important, if not the most important, functional unit of society above the individual. Chapter 3 describes and discusses the supportive role of the family in the meritocratic value system. Chapters 4 and 5 respectively describe the school system and the after-school educational programs in preparing students to be competitive and perform their best. Chapter 6 describes the fearsome public examination that is the path to academic assessment, leading

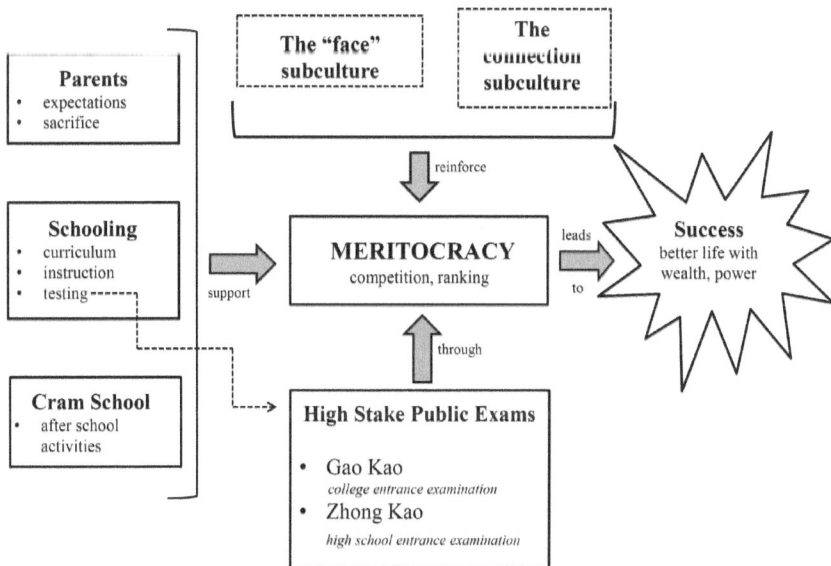

Figure 1.3. Meritocracy.

lucky test-takers to success. Finally all the meritocratic elements are regulated by the pride subculture, or *face* (chapter 7), and the connections subculture, or *guanxi* (chapter 8).

*Chapter Two*

# Meritocracy

"You judge yourself by what you think you can achieve; others judge you by what you have achieved."

### A TALE OF KAYE JOHNSON AND KUO CHU

Kaye Johnson was born in the United States. She is the oldest of three siblings. Kaye has two affectionate parents, and they taught her the value of love for her country, hard work, and creativity. Kaye lives in a good school community and attends a reputable public high school. She is the captain of the school softball team and leader of the school debate team; she also does good work at school. In her senior year, Kate scored very well on the college entrance examination and got into Harvard University, majoring in political science, with an athletic scholarship. Kaye wants to be a lawyer and eventually a politician working in the federal government, earning a good living.

Only a handful of aspiring students like Kaye Johnson, when asked what they want to be when they grow up, would answer, "A politician." An additional few might dream of becoming president. Let's face it that being a politician in today's climate is tricky, and politics nowadays is not necessarily considered a noble profession. Interestingly, the aspirations of young people in China can be different, as we will see next.

Kuo Chu, born in China, is the only child in the family. He has two dedicated parents and four grandparents attending to him like a little emperor. The parents and grandparents infuse in him the teachings of Confucius, stressing the values of academic excellence, hard work, and competitiveness.

A good education is always important to the family, and Kuo Chu spends most of his time at school and then studying after school. He goes through a system of highly selective examinations based mostly on rote memorization of facts and gets into Peking University, majoring in political science with no problems. He vows not to fail his parents. He joins the Communist Party and eventually dreams of entering government service and enjoying a good life.

The Chinese people have long believed that education is a way to reach the top tier of the country's social structure and join the elite rank of government officials. A well-known quote from Confucius says, "He who excels in study can follow an official career." While the quote reinforces the prestige and stability of serving in the government, it also implies that service to the people is an honorable profession.

The career aspirations of Kaye Johnson and Kuo Chu look reasonably similar because both wish to serve in the government; nevertheless, the paths they follow are different because of the intellectual foundations of their two very different countries. A person's philosophy can be simplistically defined as the belief and commitment driving his or her behavior. The lifestyle of a person whose credo is "Let's drink and be merry" will differ from that of someone who believes "A dollar saved is a dollar earned." The root of it all is the intellectual foundation or philosophy that shapes how people think and behave.

Both Kaye Johnson and Kuo Chu understand and follow an educational path to realize their dreams for success. Is education a process that people go through to liberate their minds or to gain better chances for societal selection on academic merits? In the real work world, the influence of education does not play on the absolute opposite poles of being ideological or practical; rather it frolics in a mixed range of cultural priorities. Let us compare the philosophical foundations of the United States and China next.

In the United States, people often debate the challenge of public education and attempt to pull the system in different directions. Some people support the No Child Left Behind Act; others push for school vouchers placing students in public charter schools or private schools; still others advocate for homeschooling their children. All this creates tension in a system that tries to educate students the best way it can.

## EDUCATION AS THE SOCIETAL EQUALIZER

Let us time-travel three-hundred-plus years back in US history and see how Thomas Jefferson, later President Jefferson, in his Bill for the More General Diffusion of Knowledge, explained the rudimentary importance of education in the republic. The preamble of the bill reads:

> Whereas it appeareth that however certain forms of government are better calculated than others to protect individuals in the free exercise of their natural rights, and are at the same time themselves better guarded against degeneracy, yet experience hath shewn, that even under the best forms, those entrusted with power have, in time, and by slow operations, perverted it into tyranny; and it is believed that the most effectual means of preventing this would be, to illuminate, as far as practicable, the minds of the people at large, and more especially to give them knowledge of those facts, which history exhibiteth, that, possessed thereby of the experience of other ages and countries, they may be enabled to know ambition under all its shapes, and prompt to exert their natural powers to defeat its purposes; And whereas it is generally true that that people will be happiest whose laws are best, and are best administered, and that laws will be wisely formed, and honestly administered, in proportion as those who form and administer them are wise and honest; whence it becomes expedient for promoting the public happiness that those person, whom nature hath endowed with genius and virtue, should be rendered by liberal education worthy to receive, and able to guard the sacred deposit of the rights and liberties of their fellow citizens, and that they should be called to that charge without regard to wealth, birth or other accidental condition or circumstance; but the indigence of the greater number disabling them from so educating, at their own expence, those of their children whom nature hath fitly formed and disposed to become useful instruments for the public, it is better that such should be sought for and educated at the common expence of all, than that the happiness of all should be confided to the weak or wicked. (Thomas Jefferson Foundation, Inc., n.d.)

Thomas Jefferson skillfully explained the pivotal role of education in illuminating mind, protecting natural rights, defeating tyranny, and ultimately pursuing happiness. Did Kaye Johnson follow an education path to achieve the ideal of success and prosperity? Is the achievement of success and prosperity through education a keystone of the American Dream? If you agree that achievement of the American Dream takes both diligent work and good education, you are definitely in good company.

The diffusion of knowledge conceived by Thomas Jefferson evolved into the modern public education model, whereby everyone receives a common and equal chance to learn. Common education theoretically ensures that all children begin on the same footing to prepare them equally to compete and succeed in society upon completing their education. Advocates of common education trust that social class differences will be minimized, as students receive the equal chance to get an equal education. It is further believed that when children of high-, middle-, and low-income families are mixed in the education process, the school system therefore works as an equalizer for all social classes (figure 2.1).

Intriguingly, the common man in ancient China could also use education as an avenue to become a superior man, or *chun tzu* in Chinese. For the common people, studying the work of Confucius, part of the curriculum tested by the civil examination, had been the express way to move up the social ladder. In this sense, the ancient and modern Chinese still see education as a social equalizer.

Barack Obama is the forty-fourth president of the United States and the first African American to hold the office. He was first elected to the presidency in 2008 and won a second term in 2012. President Obama came from an interracial marriage, with a black father from Kenya and a white mother from Kansas. Obama's parents were divorced, and his mother remarried a man from Indonesia. The mother subsequently returned to Hawaii with Obama to stay with her parents. After high school, Obama studied at Occidental College in Los Angeles, then transferred to Columbia University in New York to prepare for a political science career. After a brief stay in Chicago, he entered Harvard Law School in 1988. He was elected the first African American editor of the *Harvard Law Review*. Later he graduated magma cum laude from Harvard in 1991.

President Obama's life includes many achievements, and among the most important is his excellence in education. Who would have recognized a brilliant young man from a convoluted family background in the absence of his great success in education? For Obama, education served him well as an initial social equalizer.

In 2016, He Jiang made history when he was selected from among other Harvard graduates to make a commencement speech (see chapter 1 for more on He Jiang's speech and the schooling process of China). He Jiang is special because he is a student from an average home in a poor rural village in China. How did he ascend from a farm village to Harvard? The short answer

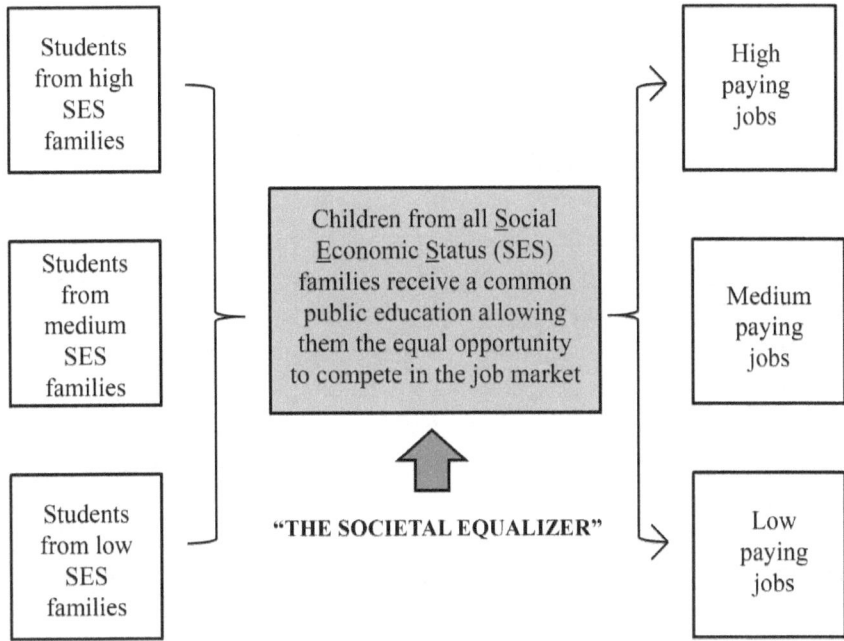

Figure 2.1.  Education as societal equalizer.

is his outstanding academic performance. Without education, no average person like He Jiang can bubble up to the surface. He Jiang's achievement is a case in point: Education served him very well as a social equalizer.

Highflyers like Barack Obama and He Jiang aside, how realistic is the idea that the common school system can equalize children in society? Let us look at one answer. People argue that sending children to a common school system alone will not eliminate differences in socioeconomic class. Why? The high-income child would return after school to a well-furnished home with additional learning resources and supportive parents. The low-income child would go to an environment with pitiful learning resources and busy working parents who spend limited time at home. Here the example may be extreme, but the debate about the merits of the common school system working as the societal equalizer continues.

Education as the societal equalizer has some merits, but it is idealistic. This idealistic model must slowly but surely evolve into a more realistic and practical model. It is the societal sorter model of education that is very much alive in China.

## EDUCATION AS THE SOCIETAL SORTER

Let us now visit China, on the opposite side of the globe, to compare the intellectual foundation of Kuo Chu's pursuit of success and prosperity. In the very long history of China, a number of outstanding philosophers have shaped the thinking of the Chinese people. We will look at two: Sun Tzu (544–496 BC) and Confucius (551–479 BC). The work of the two philosophers is still highly revered by the Chinese and scholars from around the globe. *The Art of War* represents the ideology of Sun Tzu, and the *Analects* represents the ideology of Confucius.

Sun Tzu was a Chinese military strategist-philosopher. He wrote his renowned *The Art of War* at approximately the time when Socrates and other philosophers were developing Western philosophy as we know it today. *The Art of War* describes the role of a military leader and Sun Tzu's understanding of the "winning factors" leading to victory.

In the first chapter of *The Art of War*, Sun Tzu points to the pivotal importance of philosophy, climate, ground, leadership, and strategy as the winning factors. It is thought-provoking to note the specific order of these factors: He places philosophy first and strategy last. Why? The explanation is quite straightforward. How can one afford not to understand the values, beliefs, and commitments—together comprising the philosophy—driving the leadership and its military strategies? The climate and the ground are just analogous representations of the time and situation over which one has little or no control. One simplistic way to understand the gist of the winning factors is the power of one's philosophy and its ability to define a person's thinking and action. Wow!

What is the connection between Sun Tzu's *The Art of War* and education? There is no question that Sun Tzu developed ways for defeating the enemy on the battlefield. Nevertheless, within his warfare principles Sun Tzu embedded the philosophies of knowing the strengths and weaknesses of oneself and one's adversary. All the "knowing" determines how we think, understand our surroundings, and take action. The accuracy of the knowing and the eventual action taken can lead to victory or defeat. From a twenty-five-hundred-year vantage, we can view Sun Tzu's success on the battlefield as a result of his sharp observations about individuals' abilities and the nature of the environment, wisdom that a person can apply to competitiveness in school and work, leading eventually to success.

In chapter 3 of *The Art of War*, Sun Tzu expresses his intellectual foundations vividly when he says, "If you know the enemy and know yourself, you need not fear the result of a hundred battles. If you know yourself but not the enemy, for every victory gained you will also suffer a defeat." Applying Sun Tzu's philosophy to education, Chinese students strive to discern what they know and what they can do in the face of mandatory high-stakes public examinations. Here the examinations can represent the "enemy." Students, frequently informed about their academic abilities, play on their strengths to prepare for a prospective career. Who can deny the entrenchment of such a philosophy of merit to shape the efforts of Chinese students to compete academically in schools?

Confucius is next. Despite China's very long history, no one will argue that Confucius single-handedly exercises the most influence in Chinese education. Confucius is the most highly regarded master teacher of all time. Many perceive him as a sage in education whose thinking parallels that of Socrates in the West.

Confucius was born in an era when the government was unruly and chaotic. It is, therefore, not surprising that his career goal was to change the government to make a better society for everyone. His goals for education were to produce capable gentlemen, or superior men, to serve in the government. Please note the goal of educating gentlemen and not women. Unfortunately, the societal gender preference persists even today. Interestingly, government jobs in China still convey respect along with good wages and benefits. Government jobs with the Communist Party are considered the iron rice bowls among other professions due to their stability. Is it possible that Confucian ideology influenced Kuo Chu's aspiration to serve in the government?

Confucius left us much wisdom, including his theory of society. He clearly states that society starts first and foremost with the cultivation of the individual person. He goes on to say that the person cultivates himself first and the family second. The family then serves as a model for the state and the state as a model for other countries. It is apparent that there is a structural hierarchy starting from the individual and moving to the family, the state, and finally to other countries. Lest we forget, the thread traversing the lockstep hierarchy levels is cultivation, which is the gradual process of acquiring knowledge to prepare for life, and that, in essence, is education.

The cultivation process described is the leap from the individual to other countries. For example, how does a family serve as a model for the state?

The answer is that the family must be outstanding. Again, how does a state serve as a model for other countries? The answer again is that the state must be distinct. To determine that a family is outstanding and a state is exceptional entails an assessment of worth or merits. Confucius says it right: "You judge yourself by what you think you can achieve; others judge you by what you have achieved." The assessment of merit is determined by achievement in, assumedly, a fair and objective way.

In China, what a person knows and can do is assessed through the schooling system. In this fashion, schooling works like a sorting machine for the policy- and decision-makers. Here, students from all socioeconomic statuses enter school, where they are tracked according to their academic abilities through testing (figure 2.2). In this sorting process, competition for merit takes place within the school. Why do educators think they can provide equality by tracking students? They assume, and some even believe, that merit assessment can sort out equality of opportunity for students.

Over a long period of tweaking, merit assessment leads to the high-stakes examination model of education, determining a person's future career and

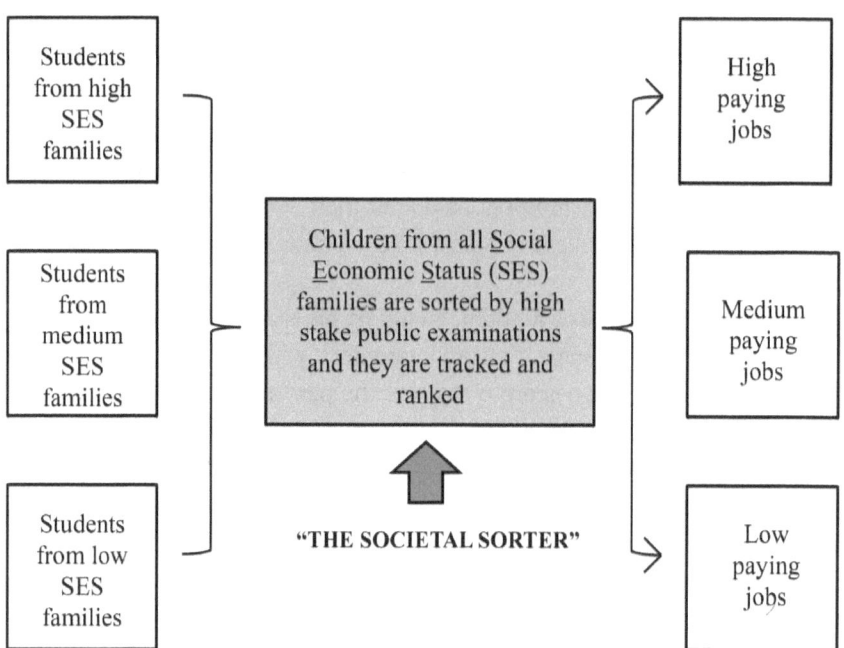

Figure 2.2. Education as societal sorter.

job opportunities. High-stakes examination begins in the lower grades, where the results determine promotion from grade level to grade level. High-stakes examinations determine high school graduation, admission to colleges and graduate schools, and ultimately employment in the civil service. (You will learn more about the intense Chinese high-stakes examination system in chapter 6.)

How does one function in the real word when education serves as a societal sorting machine? The answer varies according to whether you are the person looking for a job or the employer looking for workers. In the job market, applicants must provide proof of their qualifications; these are their credentials. A society committed to education as a sorter is strategic to employers looking for workers because they are presented with proof of a person's suitability for the job. How about the school system? The schools give students an equal opportunity to learn and have their merits assessed. Will the assessment be fair and effective? The debate about education as the societal sorter continues.

Chapter 1 discusses the big idea of success, which boils down to the attainment of wealth and power. This chapter connects success with merit. The connection of success with merit as measured by educational achievement is crucial to compare the school's ability to provide equal opportunity or to sort according to ability. Studies from official government sources such as the US Department of Labor suggest that individual merit as measured by school achievement is the road to economic success (see figure 2.3).

Figure 2.3 shows an increment of weekly income for people in the United States with varying levels of education. The weekly income difference between those with less than a high school diploma and those with a doctoral or professional degree is at least $1,130. The weekly income difference between a person with less than a high school diploma and another with a bachelor's degree is smaller but still significant at $644. Interesting in figure 2.4 are the differing unemployment rates, indicating that unemployment is lower—albeit still present—with higher educational attainment. Specifically, these figures describe the earning power with reference to weekly earnings and educational attainment.

In a similar vein, what are earnings and education achievement like in China? First and foremost, official public education data in the area are scanty and difficult to find. For that reason, one can only locate the information in public research publications, and sometimes one has to go outside China to find it. Nevertheless, we can assume universal correlation between

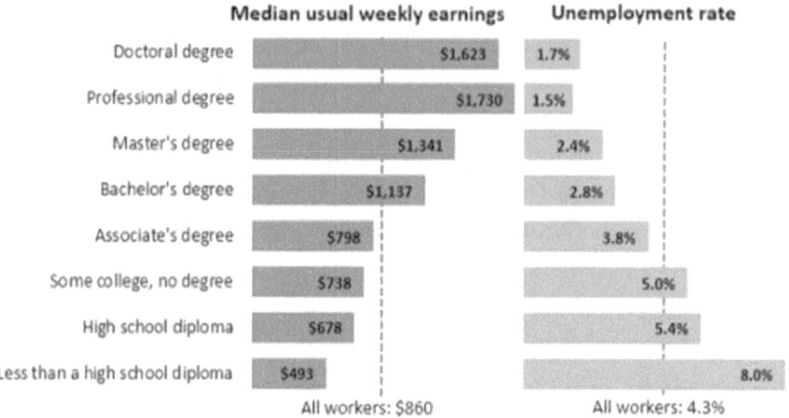

**Figure 2.3.** 2015 weekly earnings by educational attainment.

earnings and education achievement, and China should not be the exception. The challenge in China, however, is the disparity of information between rural and urban areas in a very vast country. For example, the education status and earnings of underprivileged migrant workers are not known because the head count is huge, these individuals are incredibly mobile, and worst of all some of their activities are not reported due to the legality of the individuals' migration and residency.

Migrant workers are people moving from the countryside to urban cities to find mostly labor employment. Some workers have work permits; others do not, making legal employment opportunities scarce. What is more, the children of illegal migrant workers will not get the equal opportunity to advance themselves in public schools, making life even harder for them and their families.

In a competitive world, people often ask, "What is merit without ranking?" In the United States, ranking is a part of the American culture. People rank cities, cars, tools, restaurants, hotels, services, websites, stores, schools, and so on. Here, ranking is merit based and assessed by performance or consumer satisfaction, using some quantitative representation, such as the number of stars awarded. For example, a consumer may say, "I'd rather eat at a four-star restaurant because eating at a restaurant with fewer stars is a waste

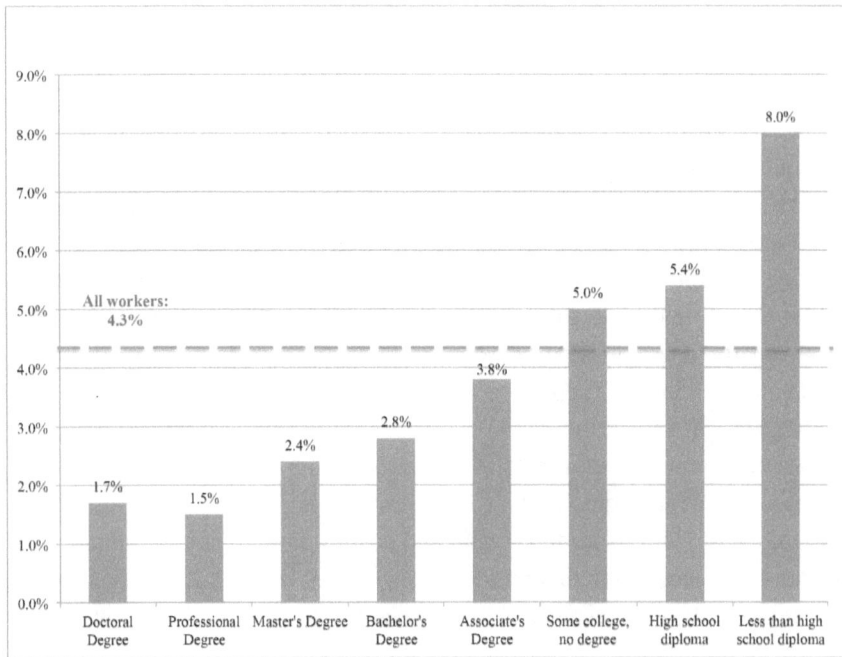

Figure 2.4. 2015 unemployment rates by educational attainment.

of time." The consumer surely expects to pay more for a higher-quality restaurant. Ultimately, the decision of whether to go to a rated restaurant is a calculation based on your expectation of the dining experience and its affordability.

Consumers understand that doing research to find the best items to purchase is not a good use of their personal time. To make deciding on a big-ticket item simple, many consumers consult *Consumer Reports*, a magazine that rates items independently researched by its laboratory. In the United States, people frequently consult *Consumer Reports* when deciding to buy items like cars, appliances, computers, and tools.

School ranking, a familiar feature of American culture, has been bolstered by the No Child Left Behind Act of 2010. Prior to 2010, school performance was analyzed but not openly; today, one can view publicly the performance of a school against the school regulatory mandates with reference to scores on high-stakes examinations, such as the American College Testing (ACT) or Scholastic Aptitude Test (SAT). Schools with high ACT/SAT scores are perceived as high performing, and the community where the school resides is perceived as desirable for raising a family. Consequently, the school community or the city is ranked accordingly, with school quality and real estate value as important determining factors. Now that we are familiar with the merit-ranking culture in the United States, let us compare that to China.

China has a similar merit-ranking culture where ranking is applicable, and the star-ranking system is also very common. With reference to education or, more specifically, student academic achievement, China's system of merit ranking through assessment is intense to the point of punishing. Figure 2.5 shows a comprehensive student assessment ranking report for a university in Anshun City in Guizhou Province.

The report has eight columns and shows only the top ten out of seventy students in the graduating class of 2013. After the student ID and name are the average performance scores of the first, second, third, and fourth years of college. On the far right are the four-year average scores and the summative rank of the student. Note that the final student ranking is based on the four-year average score computation.

How would you respond to the merit-ranking report? Different people will respond quite differently. If you are among the top students or their families, you would want others to know about the achievement. If you are an employer, it would be easy to pick your top workers, if academic achievement is an important part of the decision. How about the bottom students or

## 2013 安顺学院电信大学（四年）综合测评排名
2013 An-shun University of Telecommunication (4 year) comprehensive assessment ranking

| 学号<br>(Student I.D.) (Name) | 姓名<br>(freshman) | 大一平均分<br>(Sophomore) | 大二平均分<br>(Junior) | 大三平均分<br>(Senior) | 大四平均分<br>(4 yr AVG) | 总平均成绩<br>(RANK) |
|---|---|---|---|---|---|---|
| 201103124076陈银娟 | 86.73 | 90.98 | 90.90 | 90.00 | 89.65 | 1 |
| 201103124067林雪娟 | 82.08 | 91.73 | 89.93 | 85.00 | 87.18 | 2 |
| 201103124069梁秀容 | 83.78 | 90.93 | 88.85 | 85.00 | 87.14 | 3 |
| 201103124001吴飞 | 86.13 | 92.59 | 88.91 | 80.00 | 86.91 | 4 |
| 201103124030马倩 | 83.63 | 88.58 | 88.20 | 85.00 | 86.35 | 5 |
| 201103124020梁露蛟 | 84.06 | 88.18 | 86.78 | 85.00 | 86.00 | 6 |
| 201103124021刘娟 | 84.80 | 88.00 | 84.59 | 85.00 | 85.60 | 7 |
| 201103124015蒋祖娅 | 80.43 | 85.29 | 86.31 | 85.00 | 84.26 | 8 |
| 201103124043王涛 | 81.76 | 82.84 | 82.01 | 90.00 | 84.15 | 9 |
| 201103124064郑焕斌 | 83.28 | 84.46 | 83.22 | 85.00 | 83.99 | 10 |

**Figure 2.5.  Anshun University student ranking.**

their families? The ranking report card would undoubtedly put them to not just private but public shame.

The negative impact of the student-ranking culture based on the competitive educational system as described is cutthroat and notorious. It is truly a societal disgrace to read in the news that school-age children take their own lives to escape the stress. For many students and their parents, being meritorious in school represents the only hope for a bright future, and failing to achieve that goal is both a personal and a family disgrace.

In 2016, the total population in China was 1.38 billion (http://www.worldometers.info/world-population/china-population/), and in the United States it was more than 320 million (http://www.usnews.com/opinion/blogs/robert-schlesinger/articles/2016-01-05/us-population-in-2016-according-to-census-estimates-322-762-018). The two populations can be represented by the ratio of 4.3 Chinese to 1 American. Hypothetically, if there are ten job applicants for a position in the United States, you will see forty applicants for the same job in China. Honestly, to say that there are ten applicants for a job opening anywhere nowadays is obviously not an overexaggeration. Fierce competition in China is not an understatement, and current employment practice is selection of only the sharpest and the brightest.

The pursuit of happiness and prosperity is a race not specific to any one place, like the United States or China. To give everyone entering the race an equal chance of success, all participants must begin at the same starting line, and education is that starting line. Is it not a fact of life that some competitors will succeed and others will fail in the race even though education promises to be the gateway to equal opportunity?

*Chapter Three*

# Parents

"Mencius's mother moved house three times" and "Wish for a dragon son."

These two authoritative idioms are carefully selected for this chapter about Chinese parents' pivotal role in education. "Mencius's mother moved house three times" signifies parental involvement, and "Wish for a dragon son" signifies parental expectations. As the two figurative expressions are applied together, Chinese people understand not only their wisdom but also the critical connection between parents and education.

Expectations may be looked at as the elevated talk of the parents, and unfortunately academic success will still not be accomplished without the help of parents. Let us look at parental support next.

Parents have a purposeful impact on the education and success of their children. In ancient China and even today, people would unequivocally agree to place many exemplary parents, with special reference to mothers, on a pedestal. To kick off the ideology of parental support, there are two such real stories in Chinese history. The first tells of the mother of Mencius (372–289 BC), and the second tells of the mother of Yue Fei (AD 1103–1142).

## THE LEGEND OF MENCIUS

Mencius (372–289 BC), a very celebrated Chinese philosopher, was a fervent Confucian scholar (see appendix). The book *Mencius* is one of the Five Classics, an acknowledged subject and an area of scholarship included in the imperial examination system of the Confucian culture in the feudal society in

China. Mencius lost his father at a very young age, and his mother had to raise him as a single parent. "Mencius's mother moved house three times" is a very popular and frequently cited Chinese idiom from the true story of Mencius and his mother.

Shortly after Mencius's father died, his mother moved to a farmhouse next to a cemetery. As a young boy, Mencius liked to play with other children, imitating people who mourned and wept at the funeral procession. His mother knew right away that the cemetery environment was not suitable for Mencius, so they moved to another house near a marketplace with many shops; vendors were buying, selling, and yelling about their business loudly. Mencius liked what he saw and played with the neighborhood children, imitating the loud people in a marketplace. His mother got worried again, knowing that the marketplace environment was not conducive to Mencius's upbringing, so they moved again.

This time they moved to a house near a school. People in the neighborhood were scholars and conducted themselves intellectually and respectfully. After a while, the impressionable young Mencius liked what he saw and learned to behave like a cultivated scholar.

One afternoon, noisy children playing outside distracted Mencius from his studies at home. He dropped what he was doing and snuck out to play. He came home later, and his mother was upset with him for not studying hard. She brought Mencius to the loom where she weaved. She picked up a pair of scissors and cut the cloth on the loom into halves. She explained to Mencius that a person not putting his heart to study is like a cloth cut to pieces, rendering it worthless. Mencius learned a valuable lesson from his mother. He began to study diligently and later became a master in Confucianism who was well respected by later generations.

The episode of Mencius's mother cutting her weaving in two is an example of the parent setting the expectation and making the sacrifice. Please note that Mencius's mother made her livelihood by weaving and selling cloth in the market. So cutting the cloth may have lost her a day or more of earnings, obviously a financial sacrifice, to teach Mencius a valuable lesson in life.

The motive of Mencius's mother moving three times is not difficult to understand, even in today's context. What parents would argue the benefit of residing in a community with good schools, assuming renting or buying a place to live is not an issue? A good school district, in both China and the United States, is a community asset because it raises the value of the real estate. In China, parents nowadays still prefer to live in a community with reputable schools, and the legend of how Mencius's mother moved house three times lives on.

## THE LEGEND OF YUE FEI

Let us read about the true story of Yue Fei (see appendix) next to understand the critical impact of parental expectations. Yue Fei was a legendary Chinese military general in the Southern Song Dynasty (see appendix). He is widely seen as a national folk hero in China because of his zealous patriotism. Yue Fei had a celebrated military career in the Southern Song Dynasty fighting the Jurchen-ruled Jin Dynasty. The following story is about the loving and determined mother of Yue Fei.

Yue Fei was born into a poor farmer's family, depriving him of any formal education. He was blessed in getting most of his primary education from his father. He received his military training from a master. Legend says that he had mythical strength and martial arts abilities.

Later, he completed the imperial examination held at the capital city unsurpassed. Yue Fei chose the military career path because there had been no civil service tradition in his family. At this point, it is crucial to reference the importance of the examination system in China that supports the extreme meritocratic culture of competition. The imperial examination was the highest level of the meritocracy that a person can compete in ancient China. The culture of selection by high-stakes examination is modified, but it is still very much alive today in China, and this will be studied more in chapter 6.

According to historical records, Yue Fei had a very unique four-character tattoo on his back: 盡忠報國. These translate in English as "serve (報) the country (國) with utmost (盡) loyalty (忠)." Why is this tattoo special? Yue Fei's mother personally tattooed the message so her son would not forget it, and that is the reason it is special. Let us read on.

The societal background when the tattoo was done was one of turmoil in the midst of the military struggle between the Song and the Jin Dynasties. The turbulence brought unrest and corruption. In view of that, for a person such as Yue Fei to literally go down a straight path in life was more than a challenge. Yue Fei's mother wanted to set high expectations in the hope that her son would serve the country well, despite the widespread corruption of wealth and power. Would you assume a son would obey his mother's expectations? Yue Fei respectfully took off his upper-body garment and kneeled. This is a perfect example of how people, in this case parent and child, behave under the heavy influence of Confucianism. Other records tell of how Yue Fei uplifted the spirit of his troops in battle by showing the tattoo.

Yue Fei died before middle age, and his martyrdom became the standard epitome of serving one's country in Chinese culture. He was ordered by the corrupt government to retreat from a fierce battle back to the capital. He was summoned by the twelve imperial gold plaques. The phrase "twelve gold plaques" still connotes something highly urgent in the Chinese language.

Yue Fei was eventually imprisoned and put to death on fabricated charges. One interesting sidebar of the story is that he knew that he would be executed upon returning to the capital city. Why, then, would he go back? It is all because he submitted totally to the emperor's order and to his mother's expectation that he serve his country with utmost loyalty even to death! Unbelievable!

The commonality between Mencius's and Yue Fei's mothers is noteworthy because it signifies the noble expectations and sacrifices of the parents. The parents may have all the wisdom and guidance to give, but whether the child will obey is the critical question. With Mencius and Yue Fei, obeying the parent and the emperor was unquestionable. Here is a manifestation of the penetrating teaching of Confucius. Amazing!

## WISH FOR A DRAGON SON

The Chinese idiom "Wish for a dragon son" quoted at the beginning of the chapter eloquently reflects parents' high expectations for their children. The dragon is a powerful mythical creature that controls the forces of nature. Legends say that when it exhales, it makes clouds, and when it inhales, it makes whirlpools. All in all, the dragon is the totem of the Chinese people and epitomizes the most dignified and perfect ideals. Traditional Chinese thinking values males over females, and the aspiration for sons in the idiom clearly reflects a gender preference. Contemporary society would now extend the aspiration to "dragon son or daughter," making the two genders a bit more equitable. Let us look at two well-known contemporary movie stars and their dragon connections.

Bruce Lee was a revered martial artist, actor, and filmmaker known for action kung fu movies. Among his top box office movies are *Enter the Dragon* and *Return of the Dragon*. Do you know that Lee's Chinese name in the movie arena is Shau Loong, or "Little Dragon"? *Loong* means "dragon" in Chinese. This is where the wish for the dragon power kicks in with the expectation of greatness and success.

Lee's legacy helped pave the way for a broader representation of Chinese in cinema and created a whole new breed of Hollywood action heroes, such as Chuck Norris, Jean-Claude Van Damme, Steven Seagal, and Jackie Chan. Since the passing of Bruce Lee, Jackie Chan has slowly but surely gained international fame as his successor. Chan's Chinese name is Sing Loong, which means "becoming a dragon" in Chinese. Parents have high expectations for their children. Bruce Lee and Jackie Chan are only two two celebrities who many know.

The road to life's success, or to becoming a dragon, is long and arduous. First, the formal training to become a dragon must be completed within a short time frame of eighteen to twenty-one years: Eighteen is the age at which one finishes compulsory education and perhaps goes to college, while twenty-one is the legal age of adulthood. Second, most parents subscribe to the Confucian notion "a book holds a house of gold" and believe that academic accomplishment is not only a strong predictor of but also a sure path to wealth and power.

The historical context of the traditional Chinese society affects the expectations that parents have for their children. Throughout history, parents in pursuit of economic and domestic stability extend their hopes and aspirations onto their children. They make sure that their children are successful and support them the best way they can. In addition to facing societal pressure, children work diligently to meet their parents' high educational expectations, too. In this reciprocal process, the parents expect and the children comply, all in the name of the Confucian ideal of respecting parents, or filial piety, around the family as the hub.

Chinese parents share the same goals for their children because of the ingrained Confucian ideology and value of filial piety and family cohesiveness. Why? For the reason that family takes the top priority in the Chinese culture. Parents view family as the focus for all social interactions connected to education, and children are likely to avoid conflict with their parents; thus Chinese society is more group oriented. In contrast, American students are more likely to make personal choices independently, supporting the notion that American society is more individualistic to show independence.

The Confucian notion "to put the world in order, we must first put the nation in order; to put the nation in order, we must put the family in order" reinforces the reason parents set high expectations. Members of the child's family and community assume the primary responsibility for educating children. Would you be surprised if Chinese parents told you that they believe in the strong role of teachers in the academic success of their children? For one important reason, teachers in China attain very high and respectable societal status, unlike in the United States.

In China, parents would love to make decisions about their children's career choices and expect them to enter the respectable and demanding fields of architecture, engineering, information technology, medicine, and education. In contrast, the vocational expectation of Chinese parents in the United States is a little different, in that education, or for that matter a career in the social sciences, is low on the list because it brings less respect and less remuneration. This makes sense when one applies the formula of success in chapter 1 and shows its connection to a career in social science. Fascinating!

Senior Wey-Wey says that he does very good work at Hong Mei High School in Dalian and that means he gets As so far at a school that boasts top scores in the province. Wey-Wey jokes about the family school grade scale translating A as "acceptable," B as "bad," C as "catastrophe," D as "disowned," and F as "forever forgotten."

While this family's grade scale may be tongue-in-cheek, there is still some truth behind it. Students internalize family expectations and are expected to live up to them. Wey-Wey's parents indicate that they would be satisfied with test scores higher than what their son actually receives. Is this a high or unreasonable expectation? Sometimes schoolchildren are so ingrained with these expectations that if they do not meet them, they think there must be something wrong with themselves. Chinese parents set high aspirations in the attempt to push their sons and daughters to the top, unaware of the potential of such high pressure to result in depression, burnout, cheating, and even suicide.

China has one of the highest suicide rates in the world, especially among school-age children. Experts explain that there are several causes for these suicides. In many cases, they relate closely to fear of not doing good schoolwork, thus failing to meet high parental expectations. The one-child policy—introduced in 1979 by Chinese leader Deng Xiao-ping to slow China's fast-growing population—could also explain the rise in adolescent suicides. When introduced, the policy mandated that Han Chinese, the ethnic majority, could only have one child. During the thirty-seven-year reign of the one-child policy, many children grew up in a family with no siblings. This is another overlooked reason children are not used to dealing with difficult personal challenges, such as school or family failures. In 2016, China ended the controversial one-child policy and stated that it encouraged all married couples to have two children; nevertheless, the saga of high parental expectations continues.

Prompted by his parents, a young boy visited a community bank to open a new savings account. The bank clerk explained the application process to the young client while the parents looked on. The parents were proud to see that their son could go through the application without backseat supervision from them. At the bottom of the application, the bank clerk asked the boy to sign. With no hesitation the boy put a fancy graphical signature on the signature line. The mother from behind leaned over and commented, "I don't even recognize my son's name from the signature." The boy's father quickly answered, "Do not worry. The signature name recognition is not that important. In ten to fifteen years, people will call my son Dr. Huang nevertheless." While the father's comment is pompous, it unconsciously reflects the parents' high ambition for their son to be a dragon through school, university, and medical school.

With rigorous research, Peking University and Tsinghua University are consistently ranked as among the top academic institutions in Beijing, the capital city of China. People in academia would often call Peking University the Harvard and Tsinghua University the MIT of China. It is only natural, therefore, to assume that parents will aim for their children to attend Peking, Tsinghua, or other top-ranked institutions of learning. However, when asked which universities they apply to for admission, most Chinese students will modestly say they don't know. Why? There may be three possible explanations. First, these students do not want to fail their parents' expectations unless they have a university acceptance in their hands. Second, they do not want people to judge them according to which universities they apply to. Third, they do not want to lose face if they are not accepted. (The "face" culture will be discussed further in chapter 7.) In contrast, students in the United States are more likely to tell people which universities they are applying to when asked because there are always other options and parental expectations are usually not that stern.

Let us fast-forward to nowadays to broaden the meaning of parental sacrifice and expectations. For sure, noble expectations may entail more than just moving to a nice school community, as Mencius's mother did, or just serving the country well, as expected by Yue Fei's mother.

## THE PARENTAL SACRIFICE OF A COAL MINER'S DAUGHTER

In 2013, Keith Bradsher published in the *New York Times* a true story about how two parents in the hinterlands of China sacrificed what little they had in hope for a better life for their daughter and a better future for them when they retire. The *New York Times* tracked the experiences of this economically deprived Chinese family patiently for seven years. The report provides a never-before-seen window into their sacrifice to make education the number-one priority, with the strong belief that only good education can pull their daughter from poverty.

Wu Yiebing is a coal miner living in a small village in western China in a two-hundred-square-foot house, with only a bare lightbulb for the living room and another for the bedroom. For a parent like Wu in rural China, the average yearly cost of college is approximately $6,000, which is about his annual earnings. The family has skipped the traditional New Year trips to their home village for five straight years so that they may save on travel and for Wu to earn overtime holiday pay in the mines. The Lunar New Year is the biggest holiday celebration in China. Not visiting the home village at New Year is like not visiting family and friends at Thanksgiving and Christmas combined in America. Is this not a big family sacrifice?

A rural parent like Wu is well aware of the limited educational opportunities for his child. Some parents see little use for their child's education because of the agricultural responsibilities system. Under such a system, parents prefer their children to work in the field to increase productivity and thereby increase the income of the family. For Wu to push his daughter through school is a sacrifice. Thanks to the sacrifice of the parent and the diligence of the daughter, Wu Caoying was a nineteen-year-old college sophomore in 2013. She had gone much further educationally than her parents could have dreamed when she was growing up.

The child-parent relationship in China is about more than children respecting parents; it also reflects the traditional culture of an investment-return mentality between the generations. "Saving up crop is a good provision for hunger; raising a son is a good provision for old age" is an old but well-known Chinese idiom that resonates with the investment-return mentality. Here, parents invest early in the children's education so they can get a good head start in life. In return, the children support the parents when they get old out of respect and to express their gratitude. Most loving parents,

Chinese or American, give what they have to help their children; others just fall between the two extremes of being generous and selfish.

American parents who invest in their children's education can count on falling back on social programs such as Medicare and Social Security when they retire. The social programs in China offer fewer benefits, and despite the frugality of the family, Wu still has essentially no retirement savings. He will not be able to work hard forever. After graduation and securing a job, his daughter is his only hope for him and the family.

## THE GRANDPARENTAL SACRIFICE FOR THE NEXT GENERATION

In China, a very large number of children are raised by grandparents so that their parents may pursue their professional goals and seek career advancement. Grandparents may work as much as two shifts a day to help with the grandchildren. A recently retired grandmother (Yang 2013) got up very early and enjoyed her brief calm in the morning before leaving her home at seven to go to her younger son's house to look after his newborn daughter. A little after lunch, she went to her older son's home to take care of her eight-year-old granddaughter and four-year-old grandson until after dinner when their parents got home.

The nature of the two childcare work shifts is obviously different due to the age range of the grandchildren. The first shift is feeding, changing diapers, and playing. The second shift is more about supervising homework, preparing snacks, cooking dinner, and more playing. This is apparently a full-time job and a half on weekdays. When asked why she works so hard for the grandchildren, the grandmother explains that she wants to allow her sons to spend more time at work doing their best for a potential promotion. Many Chinese are actively involved with grandchildren because they believe that this is a way to make the family coherent and a good way to pass down family values and traditions. In a way, grandparents taking care of the grandchildren is more than a necessity; it is also a pull of the traditional culture to make a successful family.

In contrast, many American retirees in recent generations have come to cherish the freedom of not working so that they may enjoy their golden years. For that reason, many grandparents are more hands off with their grandchildren.

Parents all over expect their children to do well in school and are willing to do whatever they can to help. Parental sacrifice is an important feature in Asian culture. It is a process by which parents give up their personal needs to meet or exceed the educational needs of their children. Chinese parents are willing to sacrifice more because they want not only the children but also the entire family to be successful—compelling evidence that the Confucian ideal is still deep-seated in today's China.

*Chapter Four*

# Schooling

"It takes ten years to grow a tree and one hundred years to establish a person."

The opening idiom of the chapter is a philosophical and metaphorical comparison between growing a tree and establishing a person. The difference between the two is the time investment of love and care to reach the goal. In chapter 3 we established a time frame of eighteen to twenty-one years needed to raise a child, because eighteen is the expected age to enter college, while twenty-one is the legal age of adulthood. For that matter, one can assume that the school-age range of seven to twenty-one is the critical time to build a person into a contributing member of society. One important experience in the fourteen years of building a person is the investment in formal schooling. What, then, is the purpose of schooling?

This is an interesting question, and the answer is not always straightforward. Scholars and educators develop the process of schooling so that schoolchildren can be educated the best way possible. Eventually children use and apply what they learn to shape the society when they become productive citizens. In this respect, schooling has the power to sustain and promote the tradition, culture, and values of the society and the country from one generation to the next.

The kicker to the question about the purpose of schooling is another behind-the-scenes question about the characteristics of the society. In other words, what kind of society do we want the future citizens to be responsible for? Is not the question similar to asking whether a person needs a knife and fork or chopsticks before asking what kind of meal is being served? Is it a medium-rare beef steak on a plate or fluffy shrimp fried rice in a bowl?

In 1949, China was founded as a communist state—a socioeconomic structure with no social classes, such as an upper or wealthy class with political power, a middle class, and a lower or working class. The beliefs of communism, most famously expressed by Karl Marx, direct the premise that inequality is the outcome of capitalism, and therefore communism is the solution to the problem.

To identify China as a communist country nowadays would not be accurate because communism has evolved into a blend of capitalism and socialism governed by an elite one-party system. Capitalism is an economic system characterized by private ownership and competition, while socialism is a system regulated by the whole community.

The core of Chinese socialism can be explained by its values at the individual, societal, and state levels. People are called to be honest and friendly, dedicated to their jobs, and patriotic. At the next level, the society is expected to be governed by law to achieve social justice. At the highest level, the state aims to achieve harmony by making the people strong and the country wealthy.

On top of this unique political blend of capitalism and socialism is the populace of 1.38 billion people with its five-thousand-year of tradition and culture nurtured by the schooling system of China. No wonder the education system in China is complicated because of its political and historical backdrop.

## THE DEEP IMPACT OF THE FOUR BOOKS AND THE FIVE CLASSICS: CONFUCIANISM

There is no better way to start describing the schooling system of China other than to go way back in time because the authoritative Four Books and Five Classics lay the foundation of today's classroom, and young Chinese minds are still influenced by the philosophy of Confucianism.

The Four Books and the Five Classics are the canonized Chinese texts written prior to 300 BC presenting Confucian values. These books were selected to teach Confucian thoughts back in the Song, Ming, and Qing Dynasties (see appendix). They were the official curriculum for the civil service examinations. As I will explain in chapter 6, even today the state examination system in China is the driver of teaching and learning. So what are the

Four Books and the Five Classics? The Four Books are *Great Learning*, *Doctrine of the Mean*, *Analects*, and *Mencius*. The Five Classics are the *Classic of Poetry*, *Book of Documents*, *Book of Rites*, *Book of Changes*, and *Spring and Autumn Annals*.

*Great Learning* originates from a chapter in the *Book of Rites*, representing the work of Confucius as recorded by his students. The book expresses traditional Chinese political thoughts and the philosophy of the society at the time. Among the principal teachings of *Great Learning* are to achieve a state of balance and calmness, to refine the moral self, and to set priorities, all to pursue proper self-cultivation. *Great Learning* continues to influence traditional and modern Chinese thinking in family, education, and government.

The *Doctrine of the Mean*, a chapter in the *Book of Rites*, demonstrates the usefulness of a golden rule to gain Confucian virtue by both the common people and the ruler of the country. It sets three guidelines: self-watchfulness, leniency, and sincerity. Self-watchfulness requires self-questioning, self-discipline, and self-education, all to pursue the ultimate goal of self-cultivation. One application of the rule is not to pursue a path all the way to the extreme, as in life, work, and play. There needs to be a balance, and hence it is the golden mean.

The *Analects* is a compilation of speeches and discussions among Confucius and his students reflecting the philosophy and moral values of the country. The importance of education is a fundamental theme, and the *Analects* are well studied and also best known in the Western world.

In the Qing Dynasty (see appendix) a respected and devoted scholar by the name of Li put together a book titled *A Discipline Guide for Children*, which reflected Confucian thinking. The guide explains the importance of discipline among children. Please note that there are many family and individual discipline priorities, and education is only one of them. The guide states that the subject matter is developed from the fine teaching of Confucius to emphasize first respect for parents, family members, and friends. Second is to show trustworthiness, fairness, righteousness, and the willingness to learn. Not least is learning beneficial knowledge and skills. Note the priority of family over self and that education is considered a family fulfillment more than a self-fulfillment.

To Confucius, a good teacher is familiar with the good ways and practices of the past. A good student admires and learns from the words and deeds of his teacher, and that is respect, a very important teaching in Confucianism. Can you imagine the impact this wisdom would have in today's classrooms, where the teacher was a role model of good knowledge and the students respected the teacher? Furthermore, in the traditional imperial examinations, the test-takers are expected to apply and quote the words of Confucius in their writings. This is one strategy to encourage students to study by memorization, which is still a learning technique among many Chinese students.

The book *Mencius* is a collection of wise conversations between the scholar and rulers of his time. Mencius was a Confucian thinker and philosopher, and his topics are mostly about political and moral philosophy. A well-known argument that Mencius put forth is that human nature is inherently good and a person's behavior depends on his environment. Remember the upbringing story of Mencius described in chapter 3? Mencius's mother moved house three times to finally find a suitable environment. Applicable to education is the belief that the school environment and the teacher are decisive influences on the learning of students. The book *Mencius* has long dialogues and extensive text.

The *Classic of Poetry* is the oldest collection of songs, eulogies, hymns, and poems performed at court ceremonies and compiled by Confucius. The rhyme patterns have been studied by scholars in China for over two thousand years and traditionally memorized by scholars.

The *Book of Documents* is a collection of speeches and documents written by nobles and rulers in early history. Its chapters, with few exceptions, represent records of formal presentations as consultations, instructions, announcements, declarations, and commands. The book is possibly the oldest Chinese narrative to include examples of early prose.

The *Book of Rites* describes ancient court and other social etiquette rituals. Some rites are patterns for the family, a record of smaller matters in the dress of mourning, smaller rules of demeanor, law and meaning of sacrifice, doctrine of the mean, and great learning—the long list continues. The book, the foundation of ancient Chinese political philosophy, is influenced by Confucius and based on the premise that social and societal harmony can be achieved only by people understanding their roles and doing the right thing in different occasions.

The *Book of Changes* describes a system of foretelling. It is a systematic way to organize what appears to be random, giving insight into a problem at hand. Foretelling has formal ritualistic elements with social characteristics, and it is quite different from fortune-telling. Many used the book symbolically in ancient times for guidance in important decisions as informed by Taoism and Confucianism.

The *Spring and Autumn Annals* is a historical record of the state of Lu, Confucius's native state. The book, traditionally thought to have been compiled by Confucius, includes events such as marriages, deaths, funerals of rulers, battles fought, sacrificial records, natural disasters, and other celestial happenings believed to be of ceremonial significance.

After the flyover of the Four Books and the Five Classics, we need to note that Confucius is the author and editor behind much of the intellectual work. Confucianism has been the mainstream philosophy in China for over two thousand years, guiding the minds of the people to set proper life goals and prudently manage relationships. If we admit honestly that many challenges that we face today stem from inappropriate life goals and less-than-positive relationships, then we begin to grasp the penetrating meaning and purpose of Confucianism.

## EDUCATIONAL PERENNIALISM IN CHINA

The Four Books and the Five Classics are upheld as an authoritative collection of scholarly work; yet their real importance lies in the principles of the tradition, culture, and value of the Chinese civilization. In that sense, the learning they contain is a way to continue and preserve the Chinese civilization. In the schooling process, they support the educational philosophy regarding what students should learn and teachers should teach in school. Educators in ancient China believed that the important ideas of the books and the classics helped to develop the whole person. In the words of Confucius, that whole person is the *jun je*, or perfect man.

In educational philosophy this way of thinking and belief is called perennialism. Chinese educational perennialists, such as the authors of the Four Books and the Five Classics, with specific reference to Confucius, make inquiries about human nature and the psychology of life to emphasize proper personal cultivation through education to promote the orderliness and common good of the society. Perennialism suggests knowledge that lasts for an indefinite period, recurring over and over to the point of becoming self-renewing.

Perennialism in China stresses that the overarching aim of education should be the exposure to history's finest thinkers, such as Confucius and Mencius, as models for learning. For Chinese perennialists, the purpose of education is to make sure that students acquire understanding of the great thinking behind Chinese civilization.

Critiques of Chinese educational perennialism exclaim that memorizing huge volumes of information and focusing on secondhand knowledge, reinforced by the high-stakes state examination system, discourages the development of critical thinking. Ancient China has been the source of many inventions, including papermaking, gunpowder, printing, and the compass. If China is to go back to the old triumphant days of the four big inventions, the schooling process of secondhand learning and rote memorization needs to be decisively reexamined to encourage more independent thinking and creativity.

For ten years, beginning in 1966 when China launched the Cultural Revolution, a sociopolitical movement under Chairman Mao Zedong to abolish remnants of traditional elements from Chinese society and to reinforce the thinking of Chairman Mao and the Communist Party as the dominant ideology. One of the goals of the revolution was to bring an end to the Four Olds: old customs, old culture, old habits, and old ideas. The revolution alleged that the old Chinese culture was responsible for the country's economic backwardness.

Although the exact customs, culture, habits, and ideas specifically constituting the Four Olds were not clearly defined, the traditional way of schooling was on the hit list, as schools were abandoned and teachers publicly humiliated. Culture, the most inclusive entity of the Four Olds, is the soul of the nation. China is the only country in the world with its ancient civilization passed down continuously for over five thousand years. Therefore, the destruction of a country's culture is honestly unimaginable. The Cultural Revolution represented the darkest days in recent Chinese history, and the schooling system was badly damaged, bringing education to a standstill for at least a decade.

In a recent university professional-development exchange in China, I had the precious opportunity to attend a citizen education conference on the campus of Dalian Nationalities University. Upon entering the conference center, I was warmly greeted by two rows of young students, one row on each side, asking, "How are you, teacher?" with a synchronized, ninety-degree bow. Outside the conference center were huge red balloon displaying slogans like "Learn Traditional Culture," "Respect Your Parents and Teachers," "Be Sincere and Be Humble." These kind of messages are good for anyone, anytime, and anywhere, and educational perennialism in China lives on.

## SCHOOLING IN CHINA

Before we delve into the business of formal schooling, we need to explore the very important foundation of *jia jiao*, literally "home education" in Chinese. Home education in China is quite different from that in the United States because it has little to do with learning academic subjects such as language, mathematics, social studies, and science. Home education is all about educating the child in basic manners.

Basic manners can be as simple as being respectful to parents, teachers, and one's elders by asking them for advice and by saying "good morning," "please," "thank you," and "excuse me." Other examples include being respectful of property that does not belong to you; therefore, littering and not turning off the light if you are the last person leaving the room are considered disrespectful. Children's behavior reflects their home education and, more to the point, their parents. Home education is important because it is not only the springboard to success but also a source of "face" for the parents. A call from school about a student being disrespectful or making trouble is very serious because the child brings the family public shame. The issue of face and shame will be discussed in chapter 7.

Now that we have taken care of home education, let us ask a question pertaining to Confucianism. Is it feasible to see schooling à la Confucius in China? Yes, it is still traceable with reference to the person standing in front of the classroom as a teacher and students sitting in the classroom as learners. Confucius saw his teachings as the fountainhead of knowledge transmitted from the past. In this sense, the teacher is the transmitter and not a maker of knowledge. Imagine the teacher transmitting knowledge, which would lead to students copying and memorizing.

Visit a typical classroom in China today. More than likely you will see that the teacher writes on the board as a form of knowledge transmission, and the students copy what is written on the board as a form of learning. Put a typical Chinese student in an American classroom. What would he do? He would probably listen attentively and wait for the teacher to write something on the board. This is how the Confucian philosophy is entrenched in Chinese education. Are you surprised?

What about the relationships between people, such as teachers and students? Confucius believed that people learned fundamental lessons according to the specific role that they would play in a particular lineage. According to the world of Confucius, up and down movement along the lineage roles determined the dynamics of communication. The expected protocols in the communication exchange are as follows: The minister listens to the monarch, the son listens to the father, the wife listens to the husband, and the younger sibling listens to the older brother. Please note that the roles are gender specific, and the original role conception did not even specify the teacher and the students. Later, the communication protocol expanded to include the teacher and the student. The student listens to the teacher with the understanding that *listen* includes the broader meaning of *respect*.

Again, visit a typical school in China and observe as the teacher enters the classroom. The student class monitor will say, "Stand up." Students will stand up straight and may even bow a little to show their respect. Then they will say, "Good morning, teacher" or "How are you, teacher?" The student class monitor will then say, "Sit down." And the students will all sit down almost in unison. The teacher is expected to play a dominant, leading role, with the students following. Are you surprised? Are you now convinced that the lineage position dictates the behavior of the teacher and the students? The Confucian ideology I describe is that the students show respect for the teacher, who enacts his role in society such a way that he himself is worthy of respect and admiration.

There can be other monitors in the class, such as the homework monitor, the hygiene monitor, and the politeness monitor. The politeness monitor, for example, may report on students who have been fighting or said bad words. Students are encouraged to run for some class responsibilities so that the good behavior of the class can be enforced collectively. This is group culture in action.

Place a typical Chinese student in an American classroom. What would he do? He would probably suppress his own ideas and listen to the teacher. He would probably not challenge the authority of the teacher. For that reason, asking a Chinese student to express his opinion and participate in a class discussion is yanking him out of his comfort zone and reversing the traffic pattern in the lineage of communication. Equally important was Confucius's strong suggestion that the expected behaviors described are not regarded as mindless forms but performed with devotion and sincerity. This is how the Confucian philosophy has entrenched itself in Chinese education. Are you surprised? Based on the information, one can assume that student management is seldom a problem.

Schooling in China has been highly valued since ancient times because Confucian philosophy emphasizes education as the base of intellect and self-fulfillment. As explained in chapter 1, high achievement in education is perceived as a sure connection to high social success. The 1986 Compulsory Education Law of the People's Republic of China was launched to decentralize control of education at the district and county levels, aiming to enroll millions of children, especially those in rural areas and those from minority groups not attending school at that time. The law guaranteed the right to nine years of compulsory basic education for all school-age children to include six years of primary and three years of junior middle school. Beyond the junior middle school are noncompulsory senior high school, vocational training, and college.

Figure 4.1 shows the basic schooling schema in China. The approximate ratio of primary to secondary students in China is estimated to be two hundred to one, meaning only one out of two hundred students will move from primary all the way through. What happened? The two highly selective state entrance examinations, as implied by the pyramidal structure, provide dense filtering, allowing only the academic elite to rise to the top.

## SCHOOL HOLIDAYS

Schools in China run on a two-semester system per year. The first semester starts on September 1 and the second semester after the Spring Festival or Chinese New Year in March. There are other public school holidays such as Qingming Festival (Tomb Sweeping Day), May Day (Labor Day), Dragon Boat Festival (June), Mid-Autumn Festival (August), and National Day (October 1). Public holidays are rich in Chinese history and mean more than just days off for schoolchildren. They mean country and family in that order.

During the Qingming Festival, Chinese people visit the graves to pay their respects to ancestors. One of the best-known poems is "Qingming Festival" by Du Mu in the Tang Dynasty (see appendix), which describes Qingming as a day of drizzling rain and mourning. It is worthy to note that Du Mu's poem is mostly correct about the drizzling rainy day of Qingming. Qingming is similar to the Memorial Day remembrance in the United States.

The Dragon Boat Festival is a celebration of Qu Yuan's (340–278 BC) life. Qu Yuan advised his king to ally with the state of Qi against the strong state of Qin (both among the seven warring states). Regrettably, he was slandered by jealous court officials and accused of treason. The king eventually exiled him. In his despair, Qu Yuan wrote a lot of enduring poems to show his love for the country, and some of them are still famous in China after some two

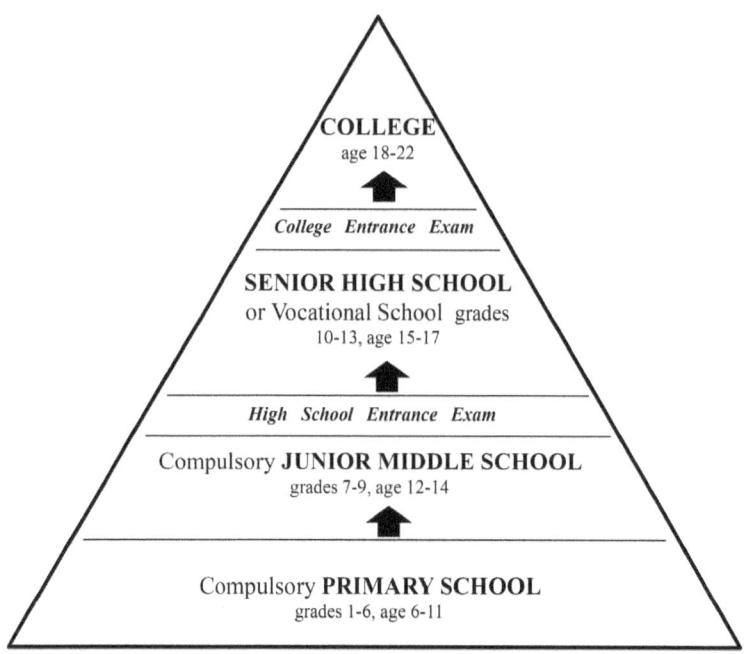

**Figure 4.1. Educational system in China.**

thousand years. The strong state of Qin finally conquered Qu Yuan's state, and in great despair he committed suicide by drowning himself in the river. The Dragon Boat Festival is not just any holiday; it is a celebration of patriotism.

The Mid-Autumn Festival has a tradition of eating moon cakes in the Yuan Dynasty (see appendix) for worshiping the full moon at that time of the year. Moon cakes are round, like a full moon. It was recorded that, at the end of the Yuan Dynasty, the Han people planned an uprising to overthrow the Mongols. The military counselor of the Han resistance thought out a plan and asked soldiers to put a paper message inside the moon cakes to remind able bodies to rise on the night of the Mid-Autumn Festival. The uprising was a success. Ever since, the festival has been about worshipping the beautiful moon with family and commemorating the successful uprising.

The Spring Festival and the National Day celebrations are China's two long holidays, also called the Golden Week holidays, as many people take time to travel and visit friends and family. Tourists usually avoid visiting the country during the Golden Week holidays due to the extreme traffic congestion.

## SCHOOL CURRICULUM AND INSTRUCTION

What do students study in China? Unlike in America, China has a national curriculum with standardized syllabi and centrally issued textbooks and other instructional resources from the ministry-approved list. The curriculum is organized around three domains distributed in eight areas. The three domains are (1) core curriculum, (2) elective or enriched curriculum, and (3) extracurriculum, seen as inquiry based. The eight areas are (1) language and literature, (2) mathematics, (3) natural science, (4) social science, (5) technology, (6) arts, (7) physical education, and (8) a practicum.

Chinese, as in the study of language and literature, is one of the two core perennial subjects required for graduation. Chinese study is crucial to sustain the fine culture and traditions of the nation. In Chinese language, students learn to communicate through conversation and writing. In literature, students delve into a version of classical Chinese study, as in the Four Books and the Five Classics described previously in the chapter. Nowadays, student will not need to delve deeply and extensively into the ancient classical works, but they still must understand the history and memorize representative idioms, poems, and pieces of prose. Many of the Chinese idioms quoted in this book are examples.

Mathematics is the other core subject required for graduation. International students from China enjoy a reputation for being good at mathematics, and the rigorous mathematics curriculum explains it. Chinese mathematics textbooks begin with multiplication in the first semester of second grade; American students start learning multiplication in grade 3. To understand multiplication, Chinese students memorize the times tables—"six times six is thirty-six, seven times five is thirty-five, eight times nine is seventy-two," and so on—in the form of a multiplication rhyme invented by ancient Chinese mathematics scholars.

Many students in China learn mathematics using the mastery approach, whereby they learn a specific simple concept before moving to more complicated ones. Students are not placed in small groups according to their abilities. Rather, students all learn to master the same work and advance as a group.

Let us look at a teaching example about fractions. The teacher starts out by asking the students to read out the fractions on the chalkboard. One student answers, "One half"; then the rest of the class repeats, "One half." The next student identifies "a quarter," after which the whole class repeats in unison, "A quarter," and the drill continues. At the end of this short drill, the students give themselves a clap—three slow claps followed by three quick ones in an established rhythm. The claps and the recitation hammer the math understanding.

In contrast to the mastery approach in China, many American students are encouraged to learn mathematics using the mind-set approach. The teacher introduces addition using two groups of manipulatives together. The students then take time to explore and explain the properties of addition using manipulatives on their own before analyzing the process of adding numbers inductively into procedural steps.

In view of the different approaches to teaching mathematics, one might ask whether Chinese students are ahead of their American counterparts in mathematics. If the question can be answered by another question, it would be whether Chinese students memorize the multiplication as facts or do they understand the process of number grouping behind the facts. The fine traditions of Chinese mathematics education lead teachers to believe that routine practice is the most efficient way to learn, and in the words of Confucius, "It is a pleasure to study and practice often what you have learned. Is it not?" For that reason, Chinese students impress people as diligent and they are good at mathematics, as vividly depicted in figure 4.2.

Uninformed educators are quick to write off memorization as a way of learning because of their bias toward creativity and problem-solving. Do they know that memorization is an exercise that retains more information, making the brain more receptive to remembering? That it improves brain plasticity? Enhances rhythmic patterns? Saves brain capacity? Helps the brain to focus? Builds the base for new knowledge? Discourages cognitive decline?

Chinese students, beyond the memorization of mathematic facts in the primary grades, are taught to understand numerical relationships. They are often asked to share their solutions to problems on the board in front of the whole class. This means students also learn mathematical concepts. The challenge to this particular method of teaching is the large class size.

In comparative education, people often reference the concept of left- and right-brain dominance. The left-brainers are more structured in thinking and excel in short-term memory. The right-brainers are more unstructured visual

**Figure 4.2. Study habits.**

thinkers with more creativity. People would say that teaching in China entails more left- than right-brain stimulation.

China uses whole-class instruction, engaging all students in the material and prompting feedback. This is different from the American way of teaching in small groups and giving individual instruction. One needs to understand that class size has everything to do with the methods of instructional delivery. A typical class size in China is fifty students, with no student-ability tracking, compared to a smaller average American class size of thirty. One would expect the pedagogy in the two countries to differ.

Initiating the study of English in the primary grades can be considered early language acquisition. Practically, an average class size of fifty students makes turning language theory into language practice an extreme challenge. Therefore, and not surprisingly, a typical student in China may know more English grammatical rules than another typical student in America because learning English in China concentrates more on grammar than speech or conversation. Students in China perform chorus English recitation, reading together as a large class group.

Outside the classroom, high school students are taught to read English aloud every morning, in the school playground facing north, before their first class. North is a good cardinal position to indicate reliability, like Polaris. This individual voluntary reading habit is known as "morning reading" (figure 4.3). Morning reading is more than the practice of language skills; it demonstrates student discipline and perseverance.

In theory, the curricular domains and study areas in China are meant to flexibly meet the learning needs of students to foster education equity. In reality, however, China's schooling system is still rigidly developed around the two state examinations, as depicted in figure 4.1, and that brings us to look closer at the instructional delivery. Figure 4.4 describes predominantly teacher-centered instruction of the tested curriculum based on the intellectual foundation of perennialism. The combination of the instruction, curriculum, mandatory student assessment, and educational philosophy connects the schooling structure to the high school and college entrance examinations.

What is foie gras? It is French for "fat liver," a well-known French delicacy made of duck liver. Ducks are inhumanely force-fed with corn and fat to enlarge their livers. Each duck is slaughtered after about three months to

**Figure 4.3. Morning reading.**

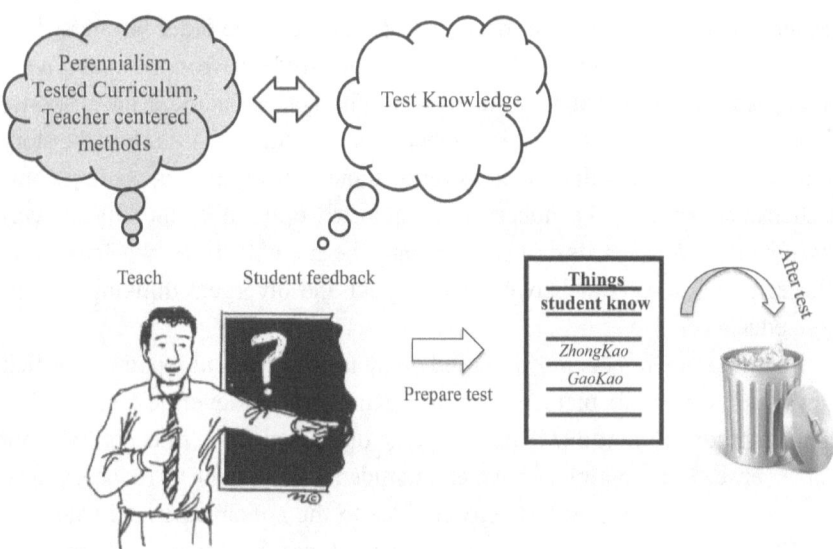

**Figure 4.4. Teacher-centered curriculum.**

harvest the fattened liver, whose flavor is described as delicate, rich, and buttery. Teaching in China is *tian yar*, or Chinese foie gras! Students are force-fed information to prepare them for the *zhongkao* and *gaokao*, and like it or not this teaching strategy is the mainstream schooling culture in China.

In the *tian yar* way of instruction, the teacher in most cases predetermines the expected response to a question and expects the students to adhere. Let us study one such example in primary school Chinese literature. Students received a short historical moral story about Kong Rong (AD 153–208, see appendix), a well-known scholar and politician in the late Han Dynasty. The story has been taught in elementary schools, much like that of George Washington chopping down a cherry tree told in American classrooms.

The story of Kong Rong reads like this. Kong Rong had five older brothers and one younger brother. One day, the father brought home a bag of pears for the brothers to share. The pears came in different sizes, some big and some small. The boys were happy about the pears and began to pick. Kong Rong, then four years old, picked the smallest one, and the father was puzzled. Subsequently, he asked Kong Rong why he had picked the small instead of the big pears. Kong Rong explained that his brothers were older and stronger, so they should take the big ones.

At the end of reading the passage, a question was asked about whether the reader would give up the big pears out of respect to the older brothers if he was in Kong Rong's place. A primary school student wrote no and gave a valid justification to support the answer. The teacher marked the response wrong and gave him a zero. The teacher expected students to follow the story line, which instilled values such as respect and sharing. In this reading comprehension exercise, the honest and supported opinion of the student was discouraged. What is described may only be a small tip of the iceberg to illustrate the tug-of-war between convergent and divergent thinking in Chinese education.

Learning in China is mostly based on memorization and repetition, which may work well with mathematics and penmanship. Nevertheless, in other subjects, the information, if not properly organized into concepts, will not make sense. For example, in America students are taught to reduce, reuse, and recycle in environmental science. Due to the nonalphabetized nature of the Chinese language, memorizing the same phrase in Chinese will not make sense for purposeful learning.

In America, in contrast, the predominant method of instruction is a blend of teacher- and student-centered methods based on the explicit, implicit, and extracurriculum—the intellectual foundation of progressivism (figure 4.5). Progressivism is the belief that students learn when they can apply what they learn and construct meaning by such learning experiences. American students take college entrance examinations like the ACT and SAT, and regardless of whether they do well, they always have other options to move forward in life.

How does one compare the Chinese schooling system and the American schooling system based on figures 4.4 and 4.5? More importantly, are we comparing an apple with another apple or an apple with an orange? The question is similar to asking whether chopsticks or a fork and knife are better eating utensils. We need to ask first what is being served, a bowl of fried rice or a beef steak on a plate. The purpose of the schooling system in China is solely to prepare the students to do well in the high-stakes *zhongkao* and *gaokao* mandatory examinations—to which the SAT and ACT are not even comparable. When schooling is based on the teaching of a tested curriculum, it will not be compared fairly with schooling based on other curricula.

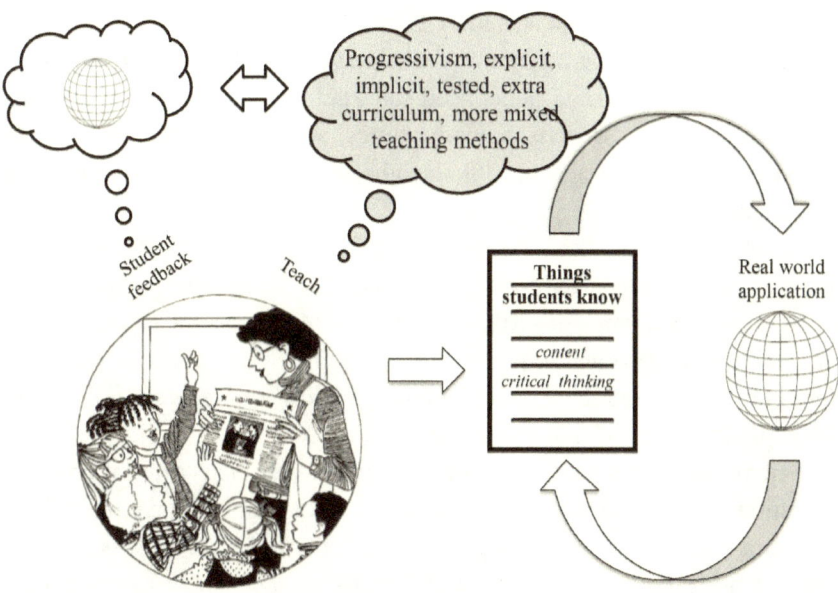

Figure 4.5. Student-centered curriculum.

## TYPICAL SCHOOL DAY

Put yourself in the shoes of Han Fei, a typical middle school student, to understand a typical school day in China. She gets up 6:15 a.m. to do her morning ablutions before a simple breakfast of rice porridge and a bun prepared by her grandmother. She leaves home at 6:30 a.m. and walks to school by herself, which is about fifteen minutes away. In China there are two ways to go to school: Students walk or someone like a parent drives them to school; there is no school bus. Needless to say, walking to school is safe and popular even for primary schoolchildren.

At 7 a.m. she arrives at school to first turn in her homework. A national flag-raising ceremony precedes the national anthem and morning physical exercise. The morning exercise occurs even at the college level. It is understandable that participation in the morning exercise in college is strictly voluntary. The older children, wearing red kerchiefs, are the Young Pioneers. They march in place while the national anthem is played through the public announcement system. The Young Pioneers are the youth branch of the Communist Party. Nearly all students between the second and sixth grades wear red kerchiefs to school every day, except on very hot days, when they wear a red pin instead. The morning school ritual is an experience about communism and patriotism shared by China's children.

After the flag-raising ceremony, the school principal gives that morning's motivational pep talk and announcement. Han Fei has four classes in the morning: two Chinese classes, mathematics, and propaganda. The double period in Chinese demonstrates the weight placed on language and cultural education.

Lunch is at 12 p.m., and she eats at school. At recess she likes to play with her friends, but her teachers want her to study for an upcoming examination. A two-hour lunch break is sufficient to have a mix of play and schoolwork. Han Fei is still too young to prepare for her high school or college examination, but here we see the examination-preparation culture even in the early stage of schooling, which is rare in America.

Afternoon classes start at 2 p.m. with geography, science, and physical education. The school day finishes at 3 p.m., but Han Fei stays for at least one extra hour so that her teachers can help her with her homework. Shortly after 4 p.m. Han Fei walks home with her friends, and she has some pocket money to buy snacks before arriving home. At 5 p.m. she gets home and relaxes by playing video games before dinner. Dinner is at 5:30 p.m., and she watches TV after dinner until homework time at 6:30 p.m. After two hours of homework, she has a fruit snack break and continues with more schoolwork until 10 p.m. Han Fei then puts away her work and gets her school bag ready for the next day. She washes up and goes to bed.

Han Fei's typical school day obviously centers on schoolwork, and the rest of what she does simply fits around it. As Han Fei gets to be a high-schooler down the road, her schoolwork will intensify greatly. She will have little time to do anything but schoolwork and examination preparation. Students spend long hours at school, and this is normal. In contrast, a typical American student will have a much better balance of schoolwork, family time, and social life. American high-schoolers might even have a part-time job to earn additional income. In China, parents are a student's only source of financial support and look upon it as a family investment and sacrifice.

Compare a typical primary, junior middle, and high school schedule in China (figure 4.6). You will find that the school day gets longer as the grade gets higher. Notably the school day starts early and finishes late in the evening for after-school activities. In America, after-school activities are extracurricular and include sports and student clubs. In China, after-school activities include more supervised schoolwork and examination preparation. It is a common sight to see school buildings lighting up into the evening.

## SCHOOL FACILITIES, UNIFORMS, RULES, AND FILES

A typical school has few facilities other than an indispensable chalkboard under a Chinese flag and a slogan banner. The slogan banners say something like "A nation's future is determined not in the battlefield but in the classroom," "Education changes fate," or "Wisdom leads you to glory." In spirit, the slogans constantly remind students about the importance of education and bringing glory to the country. Even a young student like Han Fei says that she has to be a good student, willing to serve other students and her country. Typical buildings and rural schools have no heating and cooling, so students and teachers come to school bundled up in the wintertime.

China strongly encourages school uniforms to promote uniformity, social equality, and school spirit. School uniforms include a formal set of clothes for special school occasions and ceremonies and another set for every day. Middle junior high school students in their everyday uniform, with smart-looking track suits and shoes, are the norm. A sea of students in their uniforms in the morning assembly is a treat to the eyes. To watch the students in uniforms performing the synchronized morning exercises is a reminder of the 2008 Summer Olympics in China, showing student strength, discipline, and pride. Through the wearing of school uniforms, children are taught to conform to the Chinese idiom "The bird that flies out its flock is the first one to be targeted by the hunters."

School rules are posted in classrooms and pertain to many don'ts. In essence they are about the honor of the group and the love of the motherland. Student discipline is seldom a serious problem in China, unlike in America, where one can experience various degrees of student unruliness in inner cities, suburbs, and rural areas.

The school file is equivalent to and in some ways more important than a student folder in the United States. Everyone in China who has gone through high school has a file envelope. It contains information about school grades, evaluations by teachers, test results, a college degree, and a Communist Party application, assuming that the student has one. The file is an irreplaceable record of merits assessed by government officials, potential employers, and others. A person with no file documentation is considered suspicious, coming through unofficial or illegal channels. The file serves the purpose of critically

56                                Chapter 4

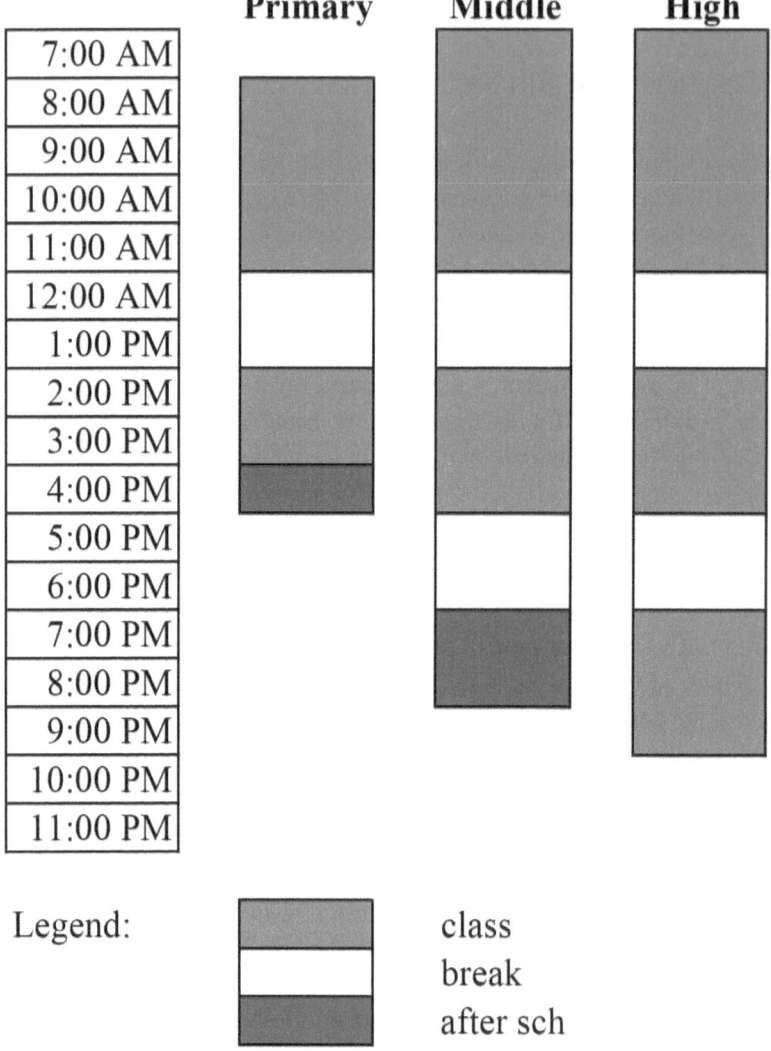

**Figure 4.6.  Typical school day in China.**

determining the worth and future of the student; it, therefore, is a powerful tool of the meritocracy and a form of societal control, as described in chapter 2.

## CONFESSION OF THE SILENT MAJORITY (STUDENTS)

If you have not personally gone through the schooling process in China, the process may seem unimaginable. Even so, we can talk to those who have gone through the process and get a view of what it entails. I had the privilege to interview a sample of Chinese international students at Benedictine University in Illinois and Dalian Nationalities University in China to get a glimpse of the schooling process in China. Their impressions about the high school experience and preparation for the college entrance examination follow:

- High school all the way to the *gaokao* is one big competition. The competition poisons relationships among people, even friends, because the person next to you is your potential competitor for college entrance and for jobs. Helping another with schoolwork, for example, is helping your competition.
- I may only be one of a handful who appreciate the experience because I would not be where I am today without the rigorous academic preparation.
- High school is like army boot camp, where your rise early, go to bed late, and study in between. I lived in a school dormitory and got to go home every four weeks for some sleep and a rare opportunity for leisure.
- Some teachers abuse and others promise. You have to be strong to stand up to all kinds, but eventually it is you who needs to exit and proceed to the next level of success—college.
- Precollege is stressful, and you need to fight for your survival to reach the next level of preparation for success.
- The last three years of high school are a nightmare that I just want to disappear, and this will take time.
- I still remember the mandatory supervised self-studying from 7:40 p.m. to 10:30 p.m. You get up the next morning, and the same thing repeats. When can I see the end of this?
- My youthful years are screwed by what I have to do to get ahead in life. Am I getting into some stiff competition, knowing that the jobs out there are not enough to go around for everybody?
- I do not think we are the only system in the world like that. I believe India is in the same boat as China.
- We have so much to learn that there is no free room for thinking. I wonder if free thinking is a threat to whoever is in charge.

If these reflections are representative of the silent majority, then how can one improve the overall climate of schooling in China? Can we employ other methods of schooling? Can we use other ways to select the elites? Can we replace the high-stakes examinations, and if so, with what? The idiom referenced at the beginning the chapter states that it takes one hundred years to establish a person, so how much more time and what other resources will China need to refurbish a schooling system to support its five-thousand-year-old civilization and "Children of the Dragon"?

*Chapter Five*

# Cram Schools

"Everything is ready except for the east wind."

## THE EAST WIND OF CRAM SCHOOLS

The idiom selection at the beginning of the chapter has a rich historical background with a deep and interesting meaning. The idiom originates from the period when ancient China was divided among the three states of Wei, Shu, and Wu. The period is better known in sinology as the Three Kingdoms (see appendix), predating the Jin Dynasty and following the Han Dynasty.

The statement, which later became a well-recited idiom, was made by Zhuge Liang (AD 181–234), the prime minister of Shu, in a fierce naval battle against Cao Cao (AD 155–220), the prime minister of Wei. Zhuge Liang was known for his wit and resourcefulness in battles. He was compared to Sun Tzu (see appendix), another famous Chinese military strategist and author of *The Art of War* before this time.

Legend says that the opposing forces were all prepared for the final showdown, and in the calm before the battle, Zhuge Liang said, "Everything is ready except for the east wind." This meant that the sails of the battle junks were hoisted, and the soldiers were ready with arrows on the strings of the bows. One important element was missing: the east wind. So why was the east wind critical?

Zhuge Liang's forces were waiting for the east wind to drive the sails so the junks could navigate swiftly through water. In addition, the arrows would shoot far with the wind, serving as long-range missiles. This is what the east wind is about, and this is what decided the definitive triumph between Zhuge Liang and Cao Cao.

Let us fast-forward to 2007. Jonathan Wong was a good student from high school through college in the United States. At the end of college, he applied to several dental schools and received zero acceptances. What happened? He consulted his parents, and they concluded that, despite the fact that Jonathan was a good student, he was not good enough for the competitive dental schools.

As a persevering person, Jonathan did not give up and decided to apply again. Would doing the same application one more time make a difference? Jonathan decided to prepare the dental application differently. He took a year off, working at a dental office as an assistant to remain motivated to become a dentist. In addition, he also attended an intense cram school focused on acing the dental admission test. At the end of the year he applied again, and this time he received eight acceptances! What a surprise! Jonathan learned from the valuable lesson that, in real life, good is not always good enough, and one needs extra oomph—in the words of Zhuge Liang, the east wind—to get things going.

Zhuge Liang and Jonathan Wong were both good at what they did despite being from two completely different eras. They were prepared to do what they needed to do and had the additional critical factors of the east wind and the test prep program, respectively, to carry them to final victory. Cram schools in China have a very similar concept of giving students the extra help to assist them in achieving academic success.

Test prep is not unique to China. In the United States, there are test prep centers such as Sylvan, Huntington, Kaplan, and Princeton Review. All centers guarantee better scores through online and in-person tutorials. The centers prepare students to take high-stakes standardized college entrance tests, such as the Scholastic Aptitude Test (SAT), American College Test (ACT), and Advance Placement (AP) tests, as well as graduate school tests such as the Graduate Record Exam (GRE), the Medical College Admission Test (MCAT), the Dental Admission Test (DAT), and so on. The test prep strategies comprise over one hundred hours of instruction, and the self-paced program can take two hundred plus hours of instruction, including diagnostic examinations plus full-length practice tests. Previously released test materials are used in consultation with expert tutors to make the preparation effective.

In China, cram schools are specialized for-profit centers that help students to meet particular goals to achieve school success. The most common goals are to meet and exceed the entrance requirements of the *zhongkao* for high school entrance and the *gaokao* for college entrance. The *zhongkao* has no equivalent in the United States, and the *gaokao* is the equivalent of the SAT or ACT. Cram schools are important because they are an important part of the Chinese school culture, and many parents see them as passports to success for their children to excel in school and later in life.

## A TALE OF THREE CRAMMERS

Hong Li was a jovial early middle school boy from the coastal city of Dongguan in southern China. Hong Li enjoyed going to school because he liked both study time and play time. Hong Li had some weekend extracurricular activities in music and English language. His parents did not wish Hong Li to cram like a bookworm and wanted to broaden his horizons instead. At his tender age, he brought home a reasonable amount of homework, and for the most part it was manageable because he attended the weekend cram school for additional help. Hong Li's parents were on the lookout for his school achievement and were prepared to do whatever they could to get him extracurricular help. Figure 5.1 shows a cram school class with small-group activity. An image of Confucius, the education sage, is on the wall just to remind students of his wisdom about frequent practice and the joy of learning.

Lai Lian and Hong Li were neighbors. She attended the same community middle school as Hong Li. Lai Lian enjoyed going to school because she was good in Chinese language and literature. Her exemplary work was frequently posted in the classroom and occasionally outside the principal's office. Her teacher appointed her a class team leader. Despite her success in language and literature, Lai Lian was just average in mathematics; such moderate achievement would not help her to go to a more selective high school later, and this worried her parents. Like other supportive parents in China, they sent her to a neighborhood cram school with the sole purpose of brushing up her math skills and preparing her well for the *zhongkao*.

Cram school for Lai Lian meant that she had less time to play and more time to study and more specifically to prepare for the high school entrance examination. What would be the consequence of not testing well on the *zhongkao*? She would not go to a top-tier high school, which would diminish her chance of passing the cutthroat *gaokao* later to go to college. What would

**Figure 5.1. Cram school small-group activity.**

be the consequence of not getting a college education? She might be able to find only blue-collar labor rather than a white-collar office job. Doing well at all the transitional points in the long and winding road of the academic path determines the ultimate fate of a person in China. Wow! Lai Lian understood the implications; however, her parents felt the pressure more than she. Could this be an issue of face, as discussed later in chapter 7?

Although an older student attending the local high school, Yan Chun was a good friend to both Hong Li and Lai Lian. Yan Chun was an average student across all subjects. His real interest, however, was more athletic than academic. His dream was to become an Olympic table tennis athlete representing the motherland. Unfortunately, his parents did not support Yan Chun's ambition to become a world-class table tennis player and instead wanted him to pursue a professional career with a college degree. His academic averageness had bothered his parents since his freshmen year in high school. For that reason, Yan Chun had been attending the weekend cram school in addition to the after-class tutorial to prepare for the *gaokao*. The intensity of the cram school classes was such that playing table tennis for Yan Chun, if he found time, was like taking a deep breath in between studies.

Yan Chun was under immense pressure to do well in school, knowing that he had no chance to go down the path to become an Olympic table tennis athlete. One can imagine his struggle in not being able to follow his dream. At this stage of his life, almost everything was about test prep, and distractions of sports were suppressed by his teachers and parents. What about his friends? He had no peers to look up to for not conforming to the cram school culture because all his high school friends were in the same boat.

The similar lives of Hong Li, Lai Lian, and Yan Chun illustrate what students in China go through from early elementary to high school. The pressure of test prep is progressive, from the *zhongkao* to the *gaokao*. Cram schools are meant to help students, but students' added time investment is in fact added pressure, and the truth that all work and no play makes Jack a dull boy is obvious in the younger generations in China. The influence of the high-stakes state examination molds playful children into compliant students, suppressing leisure and creativity. Meritocracy entails inevitable and deleterious trade-offs.

## CRAMMING STRATEGIES

In a typical day school, instruction is commonly done in large groups and occasionally in small groups to accommodate the learning needs of students. Large-group instruction is adequate, assuming student learning abilities and needs are homogeneous. Nevertheless, how effective is the instruction when one has a class of fifty students, and the learning needs and abilities are heterogeneous? In cram schools, the instructional strategies have to be tailored; the knowledge and skill delivery has to be brief and to the point. Otherwise, day schools would not get results.

Many cram schools take the following four-step approach to help hundreds, if not thousands, of students to quickly improve their grades and build their confidence in learning:

- Conduct student assessment
- Develop a personalized plan
- Customize learning
- Communicate progress

A representative cram school application form will include the following student information: name, gender, birth date, grade level, and math/science or liberal arts track. Please note that students in China are frequently tracked to reflect their subject matter ability, not their interest. Parental information—name, address, employment, and contact information, such as phone numbers—is next.

The next student learning section is similar to the unofficial school report card showing first and foremost class and grade-level ranking. The cram school staff can tell a lot about the student's ability according to the ranking status. Then there is the individual subject matter test score in Chinese language arts, mathematics, English, physics, chemistry, biology, general science, politics, history, and geography. The student may also be asked to do computerized tests in language arts and mathematics to validate the test score information given in the paper application.

Then there is the school information. This includes the name and address of the school that the student attends and whether it is a regular, district magnet, or provincial magnet school. It is evident that the schools are tiered according to student performance and learning resource support. The provincial magnet is the top-tiered school, with well-qualified faculty and plentiful resources.

The last section of the paper application includes a brief personal interview with the student applicant to find out his learning strengths and weaknesses and other relevant personality characteristics. This depiction is an overview of the student assessment process.

Cram school course offerings are extremely extensive. For that purpose, the learning needs of the student are customized by the selection of the right course or combination of courses. The course catalogue has pages of course information in a wide variety of subjects. The course can be a onetime morning session in politics or a nine-month package of thirty-five class meetings in English, politics, and mathematics. Course tuition varies from 200 to 3,380 renminbi (RMB), according to the duration of the course. The renminbi is the Chinese currency, called the yuan, with an exchange rate of approximately 1 RMB to US$6.3.

While teaching is the input of cram learning, the output is undoubtedly improvement in test scores or school grades. The student learning results are communicated to the parents on a regular basis. Cram schools in China are one giant service business in education. Wherever you see schools, you also see cram school centers just around the corner.

"The visual teaching and learning system instantaneously and clearly communicates the results of learning to students, parents, and teachers. The timely information tells the student where he was and where he is in learning. The instruction is individualized and aligned to the assessed learning targets. The tuition is affordable," says one television commercial. According to amount of tuition paid, cram school instruction can be a one-on-one tutorial—the most expensive option affordable only to the well-to-do. The less expensive option is small-group lessons, and the least expensive involves using assistive instructional technology in large groups. The television commercial is an advertisement for an affordable instruction at a large-group technology-based cram school.

## CRAM SCHOOL COLLECTIVISM AND CONSUMERISM

What is the draw of a cram school? The answer varies depending on whether you are the parent supporting the student or the student attending the school. Regardless, the attraction remains academic improvement for student success. In China, the draw of cram schools goes beyond basic student improvement to the gripping culture of collectivism and consumerism that drive and shape human behavior.

Collectivism describes how people think and act based on the influence of their peers, even to the point of exhibiting certain behaviors otherwise explained as groupthink or mob mentality when they follow along blindly. A person may wear some hip hairstyle or attire not because he looks good in it but because he appears fashionable to his peers.

When a computer user is weighing whether to load antivirus software on a laptop, what will he likely do? Most people will load the software because it's a case not of if but of when the laptop will get infected. Cyber viral attack is a real threat. In psychology, feelings of uneasiness and fear motivate people to behave accordingly.

In the cram school business, collective human behaviors can be manipulated by parents' distress about their child not doing well in school or not going to a reputable university. If the parents do not send the child to cram school, the child might miss something. Can parents afford to take the risk? The answer is no. The parents are nervous that the child might lose if he does not follow the crowd, and that is the psychology of collectivism. They want their child to ace the state examinations, which others will see as a success for both the child and the family.

A mother talked to her neighbor, seeking advice for finding a good cram school. How should the neighbor respond in this typical community chitchat? There are several possible choices. The first one is "My child does not go to any cram schools because he is on top of everything in schoolwork. I do not know what to advise you." This response may be true but is definitely arrogant. The second one is "My child is doing all right in school, and we are trying to find a cram school for him, too." The third possible response is "My child is going to Alpha Ace, and the tutors are helping or not helping my child. What do you know about Alpha Ace?" The majority of parents in China are in the mainstream school or parenting culture to support their child in cram schools. The push behind the cram school culture is the fear that the child is not performing well academically and the parents are not doing anything to help. Parents will do anything to the point of working two jobs to enable their child to excel.

The concept of purchasing merchandise or services is beneficial to the economy, and cram school is a multi-million-dollar business in China. Now that every student is cram school bound, how do parents or students select the right one? "What do you know about Alpha Ace?" is a legitimate question from a consumer's viewpoint. Shopping around for a cram school is no different than demanding a bargain price and good quality from any other product. We have previously discussed that tuition is generally based on the teacher-student ratio. However, there are exceptions to the rule. A school getting results usually charges more than another school with no track record. How do cram schools get results?

In China, cram school brochures frequently describe tutors as award-winning veteran instructors, some from the respectable magnet schools or experienced in writing or grading the state examinations. Photos of the tutors are sometimes posted in the brochures to make the information more credible. Schools with no tutor information are likely to recruit them on the fly as contractual employees. Regardless, the sales pitch of the school is "Our experienced tutors get results." Prospective students and teachers are encouraged to visit a live tutorial class before the course registration. Some tutors may underhandedly recruit students in the day class by promising them that they will pass with flying colors if they enroll also in an evening tutorial. There are other bizarre recruitment strategies; let us look at the kings and queens of cram schools next (see figure 5.2).

When people in Hong Kong see poster personalities in flamboyant poses in full-page newspaper ads, on television screens, in subway stations, and on

**Figure 5.2. Tutor kings and queens.**

shopping mall billboards, they might confuse them with supermodels or movie stars. They are not. They are the tutor kings and queens, who offer hope to students to improve their mediocre grades. In the consumer market of Hong Kong, appearance easily gets attention and attracts business. Celebrity tutors in their funky hairdos and trendy attire are worshiped like pin-up models by the young students who flock to their classes.

Do you recall your last experience in a classroom? What drove you to get to class on time? Was it the look or personality of the teacher or both? It is human nature to pay more attention to the external qualities of the teacher before they delve into the actual substance of teaching. In day school, many teachers look similar. Many will say that they teach more than entertain. Unfortunately these teachers seem boring and don't excite the students. Honestly, how many students have the decent attitude to look beyond appearances and be grateful for what teachers can offer them?

Tutor kings and queens are young and attractive. They don designer clothes, black bow ties, and tuxedos not just for the billboards; they wear them in the classroom to give them the appearance of movie stars, while blending a strategy of rote learning exercises, motivational presentations, and stand-up comedy. Some tutors may even have names like "The Science Whiz" or "The Math Guru" or some other glitzy moniker to add to the draw. With so many tutors to choose from, parents and students may just pick the tutor kings and queens that are best publicized.

Sex appeal alone with not keep students. Tutor kings and queens must have the knowledge and the teaching ability. As an independent contractor of the cram school, the tutor is simply the front, supported by a team of fashion designers, stylists, photographers, information technologists, communication experts, and, last but not least, researchers and lesson scriptwriters. To be effective, they also have full-time analysts who study past examination papers in order to predict the forthcoming examination questions. The examination analysts believe that state examination questions come in reasonably predictable cycles. The tutor kings and queens are highly compensated for what they do; they are millionaires. However, the behind-the-scenes support team gets a good share of those earnings.

How can a handful of tutor kings and queens generate such a multi-million-dollar business in some parts of China? The answer is the use of telecommunications through closed-circuit technology to reach as many students as possible. In other words, the students are not likely to see the tutor kings and queens in person. Instead they watch a lesson telecast and sometimes a repeat of that telecast, with shortcuts and tips to tackle the examinations.

One tip for taking an oral examination where you must describe a picture or photograph is to pick what you want to describe in a systematic manner. You can start the description from back to front or from left to right and add connections and transitions between the descriptions. An inexperienced test-taker might start to describe things in a random fashion, which the examiner will perceive as unorganized and award a low grade. Another tip is not to engage in long pauses or roll your eyes in search of things to say. Instead, use time-filling phrases such as "It is interesting because it is quite a controversial issue at the moment," buying time for a more direct and well-thought-out response. Tutorial lessons are streamlined and narrowly focused to wrestle with the examinations. Any knowledge or skills not likely to be on the examination are considered nonsense, and cram schools by definition are no-nonsense places of learning.

We have seen various manifestations of cram schools, and the next is the most extreme of them all. Welcome to Maotanchang High School, the ultimate test prep factory, in Anhui Province, China.

## THE ULTIMATE CRAM SCHOOL

Place yourself in the shoes of a high school student in China. Given the choice between blue-collar and white-collar work, which would you pick? It is a no-brainer, right? White-collar or office-type work is more respectable, with higher job remuneration, and is therefore considered a sign of success. Despite their intellectual abilities, high school students are frantic to prove themselves in the do-or-die *gaokao*. Many students will attend the afterschool test prep centers to enhance their test scores. The more serious ones with sacrificing parents will flock to schools like Maotanchang, with the promise of military structure and precision in test prep. There are many full-time test prep schools in China, and Maotanchang is an extreme example, considered the ultimate cram school or, more accurately, cram factory.

What exactly is Maotanchang? It is not just a school; the entire town caters to the business of test prep. It is a quiet, rural town in the mountainous area of Anhui Province, 288 miles west of Shanghai and 593 miles south of Beijing. The fluctuating town population is most fascinating to any out-of-town visitors. What happens? The town population of about five thousand will go up ten times in August and drop again during the next year's early summer months (Liyao 2013). What does it look like? Does it resemble a school campus in session during the year that empties out in the summer? Maotanchang is undeniably a cram school town operating to prepare students for the *gaokao*. The economic foundations of Maotanchang are the two highly specialized test prep schools: one middle school and one high school.

Thanks to its high college entrance success rate, thousands of parents from across the nation are prepared to send their teenagers, especially those with less than satisfactory results in the previous year's *gaokao*, to the small town to make progress. How does Maotanchang accomplish that admirable goal? This chapter has already described many fine cram school qualities, which I won't repeat here. The short answer to the intriguing question is not just the school but the entire town, which offers its students a promising life beyond working in the fields and factories through diligent work and a high *gaokao* score.

Let us first look at the school. A high school student goes to his first class at 6:30 a.m. and finishes the last at about 11 p.m. This punishing 16.5-hour schedule is even more grueling than those of other typical high school timetables all over China. Compare the regular school schedule back in chapter 4 (figure 4.6).

The school authorities modify the entire school curriculum into an intensive test prep program. Sophomore and junior students may take limited elective courses. In the senior year, there are no electives and only *gaokao* courses. More daringly, the school opens a separate building annex for repeat students—graduates so frantic to pull up their scores that they will pay for the privilege of going through the *gaokao* mill again.

School activities center on writing practice tests day after day. The school must have exhausted all past years' practice tests, leaving no stones unturned. Chances are that these students will see similar test questions when they get to write their own exams in June. How much less nervous these students will be after writing so many practice tests. That is exactly the test prep strategy used.

Student test scores are posted on prominent school bulletin boards. The regular score postings rank students from the top to the bottom of the class. Students congregate arounds the bulletin boards to talk about their hard work and compare themselves with their peers. Visitors and even parents are permitted on campus only for a limited time on Sunday. Interestingly, parents also make the bulletin board their first stop. It is unfortunate that the score board resembles a grade book on display to publicly glorify and humiliate students. Nevertheless, school staff will disagree and state that it is a vehicle of student approval and sanction.

Teachers at the school are very serious and competitive about their jobs, which hinge on their students' success. Base salaries for teachers are higher than China's regular public school wages, and bonuses based on student success can easily double their incomes. In a nutshell, beyond the foundation salary, remuneration rests on performance. The very demanding job may explain why so many faculty members are young and single, because teachers whose classes rank last at the end of the school term won't be back the following year.

Let us look at the town of Maotanchang next. The school is residential, and the living quarters can only accommodate a portion of the large student enrollment. Students not living on campus must rent expensive neighborhood rooms with a parent, typically their mothers. The rent is equal to, if not more expensive than, that for a comparable unit in Beijing, the capital city. Now one can understand why residential rental is such a booming business supporting the town's economy. So where are the fathers? Fathers usually works back home and comes to town only for short weekend visits. Many students will stay for at least a year, if not two or three, just to chalk up the proper test prep grades. The parents' marital and financial sacrifices for the family are obvious.

Student quarters are specially built to minimize all study distractions. Cell phones and other electronic devices are banned. In addition, student romance is forbidden. The windows of the student quarters are covered with wire meshing—most likely to prevent suicides among highly stressed students. The local government has shut down all forms of entertainment. This may be the only town in China with no video arcade, billiards hall, or Internet café. Students will have no entertainment for distractions; the only thing to do is to study. The school's creed is hard work, not intelligence. Is this not an echo of the Chinese idiom mentioned in chapter 1: "A year's harvest counts on spring; a man's success counts on diligence."

An old distinguished banyan tree stands near the town center. People believe it has been there for hundreds of years. They highly regard its longevity as a source of strength and wisdom. In that sense, the tree of wisdom is viewed alike in the East and in the West. The superstitious consider the town center's tree sacred, and worshippers come year-round to offer their prayers by burning candles and incense. Merchants around town sell large quantities of candles and incense to assist with the town's business. In May and especially the beginning of June, many parent worshippers come, and the worshipping smoke gets so thick that one might think the tree was on fire.

Calendars in both the school and the town constantly remind the hardworking students that the days are ticking away until the *gaokao*. The town has no place for entertainment. At least in theory, in the absence of distraction students can only study. But what about parents and the townspeople? How do they pass the time? Townspeople are likely to say that if they were not supportive of the test prep culture, they would have left town. We must assume that the adage that all work and no play makes Jack a dull boy has no real-world applications in Maotanchang.

The evening before the students' departure for the *gaokao* to designated test centers away from town, the night sky is lit up by rising lanterns representing the parents' best wishes and prayers. The lanterns, similar to hot-air balloons, rise high until they form a constellation of hope.

In the final analysis, the town is, believe it or not, truly a single-industry town dedicated to test prep with colorful Chinese traditional culture as the backdrop. For that reason, it is not difficult to understand why Maotanchang remains the ultimate cram school anywhere in and outside China.

*Chapter Six*

# Examinations

"Success depends on previous preparation, and without such preparation, there is sure to be failure."

A student in Beijing hollers to his parents, "I scored a 700 on the *gaokao*. It is thirty points higher than the minimum to enter top-tier universities. I am going to Tsinghua University!" His father answers, "Congratulations, son. Let us go to Shanghai for vacation."

A student from Dalian says to his parents, "I scored a 450 on the *gaokao*. It is thirty points lower than the minimum to enter second-tier universities. I am going to Shenyang Architectural University, but I do not want to be an architect." His father says, "Try the *gaokao* again next year and maybe you will attain more options."

A student in Guizhou discloses to his parents, "I scored a 300 on the *gaokao*. It is thirty points lower than the minimum to enter third-tier universities." His father answers, "Forget about college. Go to Shanghai and get a job as a migrant worker."

A student in Shanghai whispers to his parents, "I scored a 280 on the *gaokao*. Send me abroad." His father says, "Okay, son. Get an MBA, then come back and help my business. I just recruited another group of migrant workers from Guizhou."

What do you make of these anecdotes? What seems to be the underlying message? No doubt they are about the *gaokao*, which is students' decisive experience in life. Less obvious in the anecdotes are the geographical locations of the students and their *gaokao* performance, with the exception of the last student from Shanghai. Students from large cities tend to test higher than students from cities with fewer resources.

The Chinese idiom "Success depends on previous preparation, and without such preparation, there is sure to be failure" sets the stage for this chapter. To people outside China, preparation can entail many accomplishments, including academic achievement. To people in China, preparation is exclusively success in school epitomized by the *gaokao*! This book has so far chosen five conceptual words to explain education in China. The five words are *success*, *meritocracy*, *parents*, *schooling*, and *cram schools*. Believe it or not, these words have laid the conceptual understructure just to uphold the do-or-die *gaokao*.

## THE FIFTH BIG INVENTION

China is well known for its very long civilization, spanning over five thousand years. The four big inventions of the compass, the printing press, paper, and gunpowder are the signatures of this civilization. The impacts of Chinese ingenuity are in many ways secondary only to the advance of its civilization and modern China today. Let us quickly follow the legacy of the big four.

The compass is a marvelous navigation tool. However, the application of the instrument did not capitalize on Admiral Zheng He's (see appendix) seven expeditionary voyages to various regions of Asia and Africa due to the narrow-mindedness of the Ming government. Paper and the printing press were remarkable and may just reflect perfections of ancient technologies, such as papyrus in ancient Egypt and scriptoria in medieval Europe. Gunpowder was discovered in ancient China, and the pyrotechnic compound was used mainly for fireworks rather than weapons. The four big inventions are wonderful, but can we possibly add a fifth one that is as powerful as the original four, if not more so?

The fifth big invention could very well be the imperial examination system of ancient China, and it is the original form of the *gaokao*. The examination system represents an amazing attempt to create an intellectual meritocratic system of learning and selection in the shadow of Confucianism. A state ruled by capable and virtuous men is a cherished, albeit obviously gender-biased, Confucian ideal. Confucian literature describes the capable and the virtuous as superior. Such men are extensive in knowledge; thus their thoughts are likely to be sincere. To better understand the purpose of the examination system, we need to study its historical development next.

Figures 2.1 and 2.2 back in chapter 2 illustrate the functions of education as a societal equalizer and sorter. In ancient China, the examinations system was an effort to establish a meritocratic society that rewarded people based on their merit and not their family background or whom they knew in high office. To be precise, the establishment of the meritocratic ideal is the high achievement of the imperial examinations period.

Here is the good sense behind calling the imperial examinations system China's prestigious "fifth big invention." Historically the system contributed greatly to promoting social meritocracy. Meritocracy by examinations had deep and extensive impact on providing national stability. Why? Government service driven by the examination system could be self-reliant, despite the change of imperial regimes over dynasties simply because the system had the magical shaping power to stabilize and suppress the common people and connect them to the government like a machine. Foreign conquerors like the Mongols and the Manchus most feared the intellectuals, the Hans, because the Hans could come up with rebellious ideas to stir up trouble. Do not be amazed that the present-day Chinese examinations system epitomized by the *gaokao* just might do the same to structure and stabilize the nation.

## HISTORY OF THE EXAMINATION SYSTEM

The imperial examination system, or *keju* in Chinese, has a long history that goes back well over one thousand years to the sixth- and seventh-century Sui Dynasty (see appendix). The system became effective under the Tang Dynasty. Between the Tang and the late Qing Dynasties, the examinations went out of use for a short period to undergo reform, although the examination content remained the same.

The examination system was unambiguously grounded on the Confucian classics and on precise quoting of classical texts. In other words, absolute mastery of the Confucian texts was key to academic success. The design of the examinations affected three very important aspects of education in ancient China: first, the school curriculum from village to city schools aligned with the Confucian classics; second, teaching driven by the examination; and, third, learning narrowly driven by rote memorization of what was needed to do well in the examination. If we recast the previous two sentences in the presence tense, they describe exactly what education in China is today. Fascinating! Are you still puzzled that the imperial examination system is not considered the fifth big invention of China?

What is the examination system about? Contenders faced stern competition in a series of examinations over days, dealing mostly with Confucian texts. The core test curriculum included the Four Books and the Five Classics, scholarly works attributed to Confucius and his disciples. Chapter 4 describes the impact of these texts. Rote learning of the Confucian classics was essential to scoring high on the examinations because test-takers were expected to quote the scholarly literatures frequently; even use of an incorrect character in the quote was considered unacceptable. It is easy to understand why the successful scholars were drilled to memorize the text material to the highest degree of precision.

Preparation for the imperial examinations was extremely time-consuming because the highest level of examination was held every three years. Candidates who failed the examination had to wait three years before they could try again. Many, especially the rich, hired private tutors to help them to do well, and this could be the origin of the cram schools described in chapter 5.

The imperial examinations were very difficult because the tests covered the many philosophies of Confucius and required a lot of memorization. Examination candidates needed to follow very strict guidelines. They were required to take the examinations in isolated cells for two to three days. A wood plank in the cell served as a desk in the daytime and a place to rest when the person felt tired. The examination cell had basic amenities, and the test-taker was not allowed to leave until finished. His identity was kept anonymous. In higher-level examinations, the supervisors copied the papers to prevent revelation of the examinee's identity through his calligraphy.

The evaluation standard was very strict, and a candidate might be disqualified because his ancestors had been actors or barbers. Is this not interesting? In ancient China, people were classified according to what they did, and certain classes were discriminated against. There were four classes: scholars, farmers, craftsman, and businessmen. Scholars were at the top of the heap and highly respected. Even today, scholars like teachers and professors enjoy a distinctive level of respect. Craftsmen, such as actors, barbers, and ironsmiths, and businessmen occupied lower rungs in the system. They were usually discriminated against simply because of the low opinion of their trades. In addition, females were also excluded from the examination system due to the prejudiced view that the virtue of women lay in a lack of education. The awarding of academic titles to successful candidates was at least as complex as in the Western world, if not more so. Let us look at that next.

The examinations were administered at all levels of the administrative hierarchy at the county, provincial, and national levels. At the national level, candidates had to go to the capital city and write the tests in the palace. The imperial degree candidates held indicated their success.

Candidates who passed at the county level had the most common imperial degree of *xiucai*, or "distinguished talent" in Chinese. The *xiucai* is comparable to a bachelor's degree in the Western world. *Xiucai* holders took leadership positions in their villages and towns, and many became schoolteachers, supporting the very educational system in which they themselves had achieved success.

A candidate who passed at the provincial level became *juren*, meaning "recommended man" in Chinese, and joined the important provincial elite, with power in the provincial government. Some *juren* degree holders could be summoned to central government service, though this was not automatic.

Candidates who passed the imperial palace examinations at the highest level, *jinshi*, meaning "advanced scholar" in Chinese, joined the top elites in China's educated class. They went on to become important members of the Chinese bureaucracy. As an interesting custom, a stone flagpole would be erected in the front yard of the *jinshi*'s home to indicate his much-admired status.

*Jinshi* candidates were further distinguished with receipt of more celebrated titles, as in the Western world. *Zhuangyuan*, meaning "top thesis scholar" in Chinese, was a highly honored and rewarded person who ranked first in the national-level civil examination. The *bangyan*, meaning "eyes on the side" in Chinese, came second, and the *tanhua*, meaning "flower searcher," came third. Figure 6.1 summarizes the imperial degree hierarchy.

Wen Tianxiang was a highly esteemed scholar in the late Southern Song Dynasty. For his resistance to Kublai Khan's invasion and refusal to yield to the Yuan Dynasty despite being captured and tortured, he was a national hero of patriotism and righteousness. He shined in his local examinations and later participated in the national examinations in the capital, during which the emperor personally awarded him first rank. Wen Tianxiang would be an excellent example of a civil service *zhuangyuan*. His famous poem "The Song of Righteousness" is still a required text in the Chinese literature curriculum today.

In addition to the civil examinations, there were imperial military examinations for army officer candidates. Candidates were tested on horseback riding and their expertise in using ancient Chinese weapons such as the bow

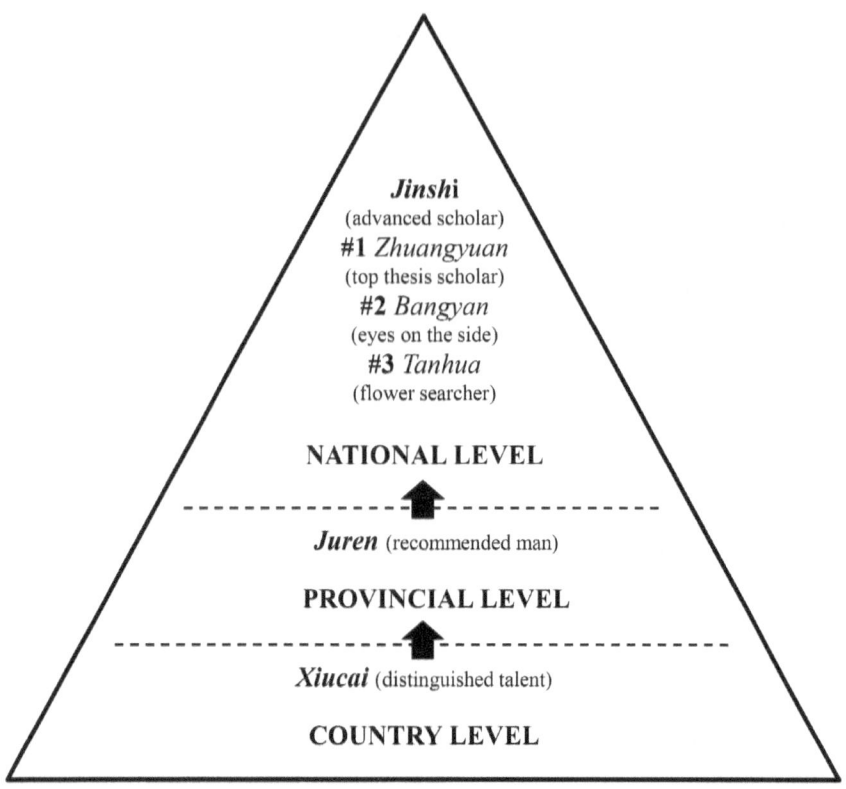

**Figure 6.1. The *gaokao* structure.**

and arrow, spear, double-edged straight sword, shield, axe-shaped arm, crossbow, single-edged sword, staff, battle axe, and halberd. As with the civil examinations, successful candidates received military titles and honors. Yue Fei, a very well-known military legend in ancient China who achieved the military *zhuangyuan*, is described in chapter 3.

Depending on the dynasty, court officials used various forms of attire, including necklaces, hats, and badges, to indicated the academic title received. Is not the flamboyant court attire described similar to the equally colorful academic gown and hood of the United States? In a way, the *zhuangyuan* and *bangyan*, the two highest academic titles, are remotely similar to the valedictorian and salutatorian in the US academic system. Other comparative education scholars liken the *zhuangyuan* to the PhD degree in the United States. Honestly, this is not correct because in ancient China there was only one *zhuangyuan* every three years. Regardless of what comparisons we wish to draw, the rigor of the Chinese imperial examination system was second to none.

After successful completion of the examinations, the individual would be recruited to work in various government departments to collect taxes, serve as judges, enforce laws, and keep the census; the highest ranks lived in the palace and reported directly to the emperor. Many of the successful were just common people with humble backgrounds, but they all ended up as the early version of the Chinese elites. Even today, government employment is prestigious and a career ideal for many. Could this be the ancestral form of the rich and famous?

## FRAMEWORK OF THE EXAMINATION

The subject selection of the *gaokao* follows two tracks, either the arts or the sciences, with shared compulsory subjects (figure 6.2). The three shared compulsory subjects are Chinese literature, mathematics, and a foreign language. The foreign language is usually English. The three subjects in the arts track are history, politics, and geography. The three subjects in the science track are physics, chemistry, and biology. A student who selects the science track must take a relatively harder mathematics test that includes calculus, which is not required for those on the arts track.

The shared compulsory subjects are worth 150 points each, and arts and science track courses are worth 100 points each. The highest possible score on the *gaokao* is 750 points. By design, students from China's fifty-five ethnic minorities, or the non-Han Chinese, also automatically get points added to their scores. This is an amazing *gaokao* policy to help minority students succeed.

The *gaokao* subject selection structure shown in figure 6.2 is commonly known as the "3 + $x$" system. The "3" represents the three shared compulsory subjects, and the $x$ is the number of track subjects. The "3 + $x$" is commonly implemented in most parts of the country, from Beijing and Shanghai to Inner Mongolia and Tibet. In recent years, one can see different forms of examinations in various provinces due to variation in arts or science subject selection.

# GAOKAO
(Total score = *750*)

| Compulsory Subjects: |
|---|
| Chinese Literature , Mathematics , Foreign Language |
| (*150*) (*150*) (*150*) |

"and"

| Arts Track: | "or" | Science Track: |
|---|---|---|
| • History (*100*)<br>• Politics (*100*)<br>• Geography (*100*) | | • Chemistry (*100*)<br>• Physics (*100*)<br>• Biology (*100*) |

Figure 6.2. Subject selection for *gaokao*.

MATHEMATICS QUESTION SAMPLER

The extremely complex *gaokao* mathematics curriculum is compulsory for both arts and science track students (figure 6.2). The mathematics questions cover computation, estimation, algebra, geometry, trigonometry, probability, statistics, estimation, and word problems. The two sample questions (Beijing Tianli Examination Information Network 2015) exhibited in figures 6.3 and 6.4 are for the science track students. The complexity of these sample questions is higher than comparable questions for the arts track students. In China *gaokao* students are not permitted to use calculators, whereas in the United States students can use calculators for the American College Testing and Scholastic Aptitude Test mathematics portions. What a difference between the East and the West!

There is a function $f(x) = \frac{1}{x}$, $g(x) = ax^2 + bx (a, b \in R, a \neq 0)$. If the graph of y= $f(x)$ and the graph of y= $g(x)$ just have two different intersections A($x_1, y_1$) and B($x_2, y_2$), then which of the following statements are true?

(A)  When $a < 0$, $x_1 + x_2 < 0, y_1 + y_2 > 0$
(B)  When $a < 0$, $x_1 + x_2 > 0, y_1 + y_2 < 0$
(C)  When $a > 0$, $x_1 + x_2 < 0, y_1 + y_2 < 0$
(D)  When $a > 0$, $x_1 + x_2 > 0, y_1 + y_2 > 0$

**Figure 6.3. Mathematics sample question 1.**

In the graph, ABDC is an isosceles trapezium. AB // CD, ∠DAB=60°, FC ⊥ Plane ABCD, AE ⊥ BD and CB=CD=CF.

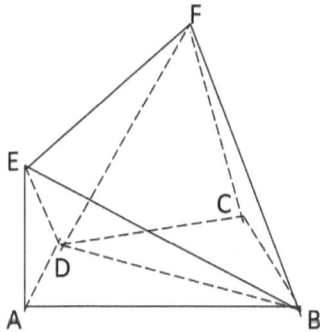

(1) Proof the BD ⊥ Plane AED:

(2) What is the cosine value of the two-planes-angle F-BD-C?

**Figure 6.4. Mathematics sample question 2.**

## ENGLISH QUESTION SAMPLER

It is next to impossible to review all the *gaokao* examination questions, as they are so diverse and extensive. I will look at only four types of English question samples: English usage, listening comprehension, reading comprehension, and writing. These questions are authentic in that they are questions from previous years that were publicly released as study questions.

The first section of the English examination is English usage. Students read a sentence and choose the best word for each blank, marking *a, b, c,* or *d* on the answer sheet. Please note that, due to space limitations, only the first five questions are shown from the entire fourteen (Beijing Tianli Examination Information Network 2015):

(1) I got the job I wanted at the public library. _____! That's good news.
    (a) Go ahead (b) Cheers (c) Congratulations (d) Come on
(2) It is quite hot today. Do you feel like _____ for a swim?
    (a) to go (b) going (c) go (d) having gone
(3) Please send us all the information _____ you have about the candidate for the position.
    (a) that (b) which (c) as (d) what
(4) The Scottish girl _____ blue eyes won the first prize in the Fifth Chinese Speech Contest.
    (a) by (b) of (c) in (d) with
(5) _____ the delayed flight will take off depends much on the weather.
    (a) Why (b) When (c) That (d) What

The second section of the English examination is listening comprehension. Students listen to an audio tape with five conversational exchanges and answer questions (Tian Li National Gaokao Exam Questions Research Center 2015).

(1) What does the woman want to do?
    (a) Find a place. (b) Buy a map. (c) Get an address.
(2) What will the man do for the woman?
    (a) Repair her car. (b) Give her a ride. (c) Pick up her aunt.
(3) Who might Mr. Peterson be?
    (a) A new professor (b) A department head (c) A company director
(4) What does the man think of the book?
    (a) Quite difficult (b) Very interesting (c) Too simple
(5) What are the speakers talking about?
    (a) Weather (b) Clothes (c) News

The third section of the English examination is reading comprehension. Students select the best answer in the multiple-choice format. Each correct answer is worth two points. The reading passage follows:

Walt Disney is credited for creating such wonderful things as Donald Duck and Mickey Mouse. However, he cannot take the credit for creating other well-loved characters, such as Cinderella and Snow White. **They** are almost automatically associated with Disney because Disney turned old fables into cartoon movies.

The original Cinderella varies very much from the Disney version we know today. It started off with the girl mourning her mother's death and going to her tomb three times a day. In addition, there were birds that helped Cinderella; there was no such thing as a fairy godmother or helpful mice, nor was there mention of a horse and carriage.

The stepsisters were cruel: they always threw Cinderella's food into the ashes of the fire, and made her sleep on the ashes on the floor, hence her name.

In the original story, the king's ball actually lasted for three days. With the help of the birds, the girl, beautifully dressed, danced with the prince on all three nights and the prince fell in love with her. However, she broke away from him to rush back home each night. On the last night, the prince placed something sticky on the stairs; as Cinderella made her escape, a shoe got stuck on it.

Here now is where the story becomes unpleasant: when the prince went to the house looking for the girl whose foot fit the shoe, the wicked stepmother told one of her two daughters to cut off her big toe to fit into the shoe. The daughter did as told. So the prince took her away to be his bride. But, when they passed the tomb of Cinderella's mother, the birds called out to the prince.

Turn and peep, there's blood in the shoe; the shoe is too small, the true bride waits for you. Realizing that he had been tricked, the prince returned the daughter to her mother; the other had to cut off part of her heel In order to fit into the shoes, with the same result. Only Cinderella's foot fit perfectly and so the prince chose to marry her. The story ends with the wedding day. As Cinderella's two stepsisters followed her, pretending to be devoted to her so that they could enjoy the king's riches, two birds flew by and plucked out their eyes. Because of their wickedness and falsehood, they had to spend the rest of their days blind.

The original Cinderella is so different from the Disney version. Thank goodness Disney made such changes; it indeed was a wise move. (Tian Li National Gaokao Exam Questions Research Center 2015)

(1) What does the bold word "They" in the first paragraph refer to?
　(a) Wonderful things (b) Well-loved characters (c) Old fables (d) Cartoon movies
(2) How did Cinderella get her name?

(a) The birds come up with it. (b) It was given by Disney. (c) It came from the word "ash." (d) She got it from her mother.
(3) Which of the following is true according to the original story?
(a) Helpful mice got Cinderella a beautiful dress. (b) The ball was held to celebrate the prince's wedding. (c) Cinderella left the shoe on the stair on purpose. (d) The birds told the prince that he had been cheated.
(4) The moral of the story is that _____.
(a) a wicked person cannot escape punishment (b) a devoted person certainly deserves respect (c) a well-behaved child earns a great reward (d) a dishonest child cannot get her mother's love
(5) What does the author think of the Disney version?
(a) Excellent (b) Ordinary (c) Dull (d) Ridiculous

The fourth section of the English examination is writing. Here are the instructions:

> Assume you are Li Hua and you plan to attend a summer language institute in England. A newspaper advertisement (figure 6.5) got your interest. Please write a letter of approximately one hundred words to ask the institution for more information.

## KNOCKING EXAMINATIONS

Are the rich better able to afford the education needed to pass the examinations? One would assume so because only the rich can come up with the money for better schools and private tutors. For that reason, students from big cities like Beijing and Shanghai tend to have higher examination-passage rates; therefore the anecdotes at the beginning of the chapter are not altogether fictitious. Critics say that the examinations are biased against the poor, who have fewer resources to pursue their education dreams.

The meritocratic nature of the examinations encourages common students to aspire, but the system can also be a source of frustration and bitterness for the less successful. How can an inflexible system that relies so much on rote learning provide opportunities for intelligent and creative individuals to better themselves? Many who fail in this system will leave unfulfilled and angry. A popular Chinese adage says, "A knife does not have two sharp edges," meaning that no system will please everyone. Some will win, others will lose, and that is a fact of life.

> **ENJOY A RELAXING STUDY BREAK IN BEAUTIFUL LANCASTER**
>
> Language Centre and College of Arts
> Lancaster University
>
>
>
> Languages, English, French, Spanish
> Arts, Politics, Sociology, History
> \*\*
> 3 week, 6 week, and 12 week courses
> \*\*
> Reasonable fees
> \*\*
> Accommodation service

**Figure 6.5. Study abroad advertisement.**

Cheating on high-stakes examinations is reported everywhere, and China is no exception. Psychologists explain that today's students live in a culture that more than ever fosters the temptation to cheat. The chief reason is the increased emphasis on testing, which becomes a part of the learning culture. Success in school today depends on a host of examinations, often starting as early as primary school and continuing throughout high school. Those tests determine where young people will seek employment or go to college, and most believe that in a progressively competitive world, college degrees plus work experience eventually determine success.

It is unfortunate that students in China tend to focus more on the *gaokao* score than on learning and self-improvement. Who can blame them? Subconsciously, students develop a rigid idea of what they want to do in school. In other words, they see schooling not as a process to foster growth and learning but as a means to demonstrate knowledge and ability by way of test results. The examinations system in China, as in other places with similar systems, creates an environment that tempts test-takers to cheat.

A visit to a *gaokao* test site is eye-opening. You see for yourself SWAT teams guarding sealed examination papers, with military police controlling crowds so that they do not cause trouble. In addition, surveillance drones and metal detectors are deployed to catch those smuggling in illegal electronic equipment, while iris and fingerprint scanners flush out brainy impersonators paid to write the test in lieu of the bona fide test-taker. How much would the security measures stress the test-takers, and where would you find such tight examination security outside China?

Would you believe that Chinese students may face up to seven years in prison for cheating on the *gaokao*? The punishment may not fit the crime, but Chinese law enforcers believe that only harsh punishment will stop the undesirable behavior immediately. The Chinese idiom "Kill the chicken to scare the monkey" is fitting here because it suggests making an example out of one cheater to warn other cheaters. Sometimes you wonder how the rest of the world deals with the same problem if cheating on the *gaokao* in China is a criminal offense.

Suicide is an increasing problem in China, and it has been the leading cause of death for school-age children. What do you make of a higher suicide rate in the second half of the school year? Is it possible that students experience more stress due to end-of-term final examinations, the high school entrance examination, and the college entrance examination? It is not even news that the biggest perpetrator of student stress is the *gaokao*. How can students not be stressed if they have only a single shot at the yearly examinations? Score results are an ordeal for whole families, who often pin high hopes on what are for many their only child.

Many people offer help or suggest ways to reduce cheating and suicide, such as school counseling and assistance hotlines. Will more communication among students, teachers, and parents help? A common Chinese saying states it well: "How can one change the consequence if you change the water but not the medicine?" Traditional Chinese herbal medicine is prepared by boiling herbs in water, like soup. For that reason, a suggestion to solve a problem is futile if it is just to change the water. The real change should be to the medicine, which is the cutthroat examination system. Realistically, determining what China can replace the examinations system with is the real challenge.

The idiom selection at the beginning of the chapter—"Success depends on previous preparation, and without such preparation, there is sure to be failure"—points to a narrow kind of preparation in China. That preparation for examinations leads to the competitive selection of students, leading to success in life.

The following lists how examination preparation connects to the big picture of chapters 1 through 5:

1. It is a long and winding path to success.
2. It is the process of meritocracy.
3. Parents support the process under the system.
4. Schools adhere to the examination curriculum in their instruction.
5. Cram school instruction is aligned with the examination curriculum to give students the edge.

*Chapter Seven*

# Face

"Men cannot live without a face, and trees cannot live without bark."

Why do people behave the way they do? The answer is not always straightforward because the cause can blend the person's situation, experience, and culture. Apart from the stimulus response theory of psychology, experience and culture explain the triggering mechanism of behavior. If human behavior is a floating iceberg, then experience and culture comprise the submerged portion. The top portion of the iceberg could not exist without its submerged base. The opening idiom explains it well: "Men cannot live without a face." Face, or *lian* in Chinese, is a fairly abstract concept whose full explanation necessitates many examples. This chapter looks at issues that confront the Chinese nation, society, and family with specific reference to education.

## CONFRONTING, LOSING, AND GAINING FACE IN 200+ YEARS

In 1793, George Macartney was the first British envoy to visit China, opening the first official contact between the Lion and the Dragon in modern history. The Macartney mission was prompted by restrictive Chinese trade regulations and the British demand for tea, porcelain, silk, and like merchandise from China. In return for these products, the Chinese government wanted payment in silver. A trade deficit slowly developed due to the business aspects of supply and demand. To address the deficit, efforts were made to find something that could be sold to the Chinese. That something was tragically opium, an addictive drug for recreational use.

The major mission of the Macartney visit was to expand trade relations, procure a small coastal island in China for British merchants, and establish a British embassy in Beijing, the capital city. History chronicled that the Macartney mission was a failure. From another perspective, it was not a total failure after all because precious cultural, geographical, and political information about China not known to the rest of the world at that time was documented and brought back to Europe. Through these records, people from outside the Middle Kingdom learned about how the Chinese and even Emperor Qianlong (see appendix) behaved, because face was the driving force behind their actions.

Macartney brought with him from Britain gifts such as clocks, telescopes, air guns, and other technological marvels of the Industrial Revolution. Macartney had every reason to believe that the emperor of China would be interested in all these amazing gadgets and flattered by the well-staffed delegation of diplomats, scientists, musicians, painters, priests, and more. He could not imagine that the emperor would not view his gifts as precious. It did not take Macartney too long to find out that the Qing emperor was not impressed. He was infuriated by the gift of clocks. Why? Chinese do not give clocks because the Chinese pronunciation of "giving/sending clocks" is the same as "paying tribute to the dead"; therefore the gift of clocks is seen as a deadly curse.

The ritual of three kneelings and nine bowings as dictated by court protocol further crumbled the ambassadorial relationship. The person bowing must have both knees on the floor. Furthermore, the bow is so deep that the forehead touches the floor. Macartney was prepared to tip his hat, go down on one knee, and even kiss the emperor's hand, if needed, but he refused to follow the ritual, and the rest is history. This segment of history is a fascinating example of a face confrontation between Lord Macartney and Emperor Qianlong, each representing not just his country but also his pride. Who was right and who was wrong? In a situational face confrontation, the matter is not about right or wrong but about whom or what each person represents.

Qianlong was highly regarded in Chinese history as a great and long-reigning emperor. The then-egocentric country felt strong and wealthy enough to dazzle any equals in the ancient world. In 1793, Qianlong issued a decree to the king of Britain, George III, not knowing that it would change the course of China's modern history. The historical decree read, "Our dynasty's majestic virtue has penetrated unto every country under Heaven, and kings of all nations have offered their costly tribute by land and sea. As your ambassador can see for himself, we possess all things. I set no value on objects strange or ingenious, and have no use for your country's manufactures. This then is my answer to your request to appoint a representative at my court, a request contrary to our dynastic usage, which would only result in inconvenience to yourself" (Halsall 1997).

Earlier a trade deficit was mentioned between Britain and China; it arose because Britain's ability to purchase with silver was weakening. The British traders smuggled opium into China and used the drug instead of silver to pay for goods. Lo and behold, opium slowly but surely became a severe problem. The nation was becoming addicted.

The increasing number of opium addicts alarmed the Chinese government, which took decisive action to suppress and halt the opium trade. In 1839, Viceroy Lin Zexu (see appendix) arrested opium merchants, confiscated and destroyed chests of British opium, and later blockaded the sea port from European ships. Given no alternatives, the British decided to open China by force. In 1840, the British launched what would turn into the Opium Wars against China, and the long isolation of the Middle Kingdom began.

The war ended with the Treaty of Nanking in 1842 and the surrender of the island of Hong Kong to Britain. The Chinese deemed the Treaty of Nanking unequal because it gave Britain no obligations and was far from mutual. As a result of the conflict, China lost face for the first time and for a long time afterward because she realized that the Middle Kingdom was no match for the military might of the foreign barbarians. The defeat of China, in addition to the loss of properties and other material goods, represented a loss of face in the eyes of the world. In this sense, the loss of face conveys the loss of pride and calculation and a feeling of incompetence and defeat. How would a person—and in this case a country—respond after such a loss of face? Let us find out in the next period of Chinese history.

Between 1894 and 1895, a conflict between China and Japan erupted primarily over the control of Korea. This is known as the First Sino-Japanese War. The conflict demonstrated the failure of the Qing Dynasty to modernize its military to fend off menaces to its sovereignty; subsequently, dominance in the region shifted. China's prestige suffered a major blow when Korea became a protectorate state of Japan. This humiliation was another loss of face from big China to small Japan.

The Second Sino-Japanese War was a military conflict fought between the Republic of China and the Empire of Japan from 1937 to 1945. It stemmed from Japan's imperialist policy to expand its political influence to gain access to resources in the Asia-Pacific region. China was at the bottom of the pile when defeated on her home turf, and the massacre at Nanking was one atrocity that would boil the blood of any human. After the sneak attack on Pearl Harbor by the Japanese, the Sino-Japanese War merged with World War II. Japan finally surrendered in 1945 after the bombing of Hiroshima and Nagasaki. Despite the severe war damage by the Japanese, China was eventually declared a World War II victor with the Allied forces.

This part of the chapter is not meant to recount the modern history of China; however, it illustrates a nation's struggle with confrontation and the loss of face to other world powers. To the Chinese, it is less about threat than about history; it is about never again; it is about face. China's feet had been held to the fire, and it is interesting to see how she reflected, regrouped, and responded as we turn to the next section of the history book.

Face is not always best saved through hostile conflicts causing property damage and pointless loss of life. What would be an alternative? Almost three thousand years ago, the Greeks founded a series of athletic competitions among representatives of city-states of ancient Greece, held every four years. It was widely written that, during the games, all conflicts among the states in competition were postponed until the games were finished. Would not the Olympic Games be a good alternative to settle face disputes?

The modern Olympic Games are an acclaimed international event celebrating the ideal of friendly competition and promoting world peace and unity. The five interlinked rings of blue, yellow, black, green, and red on the Olympic flag represent the five continents of Africa, America, Asia, Oceania, and Europe. The flag is symbolic of the diversity and unity of the participating athletes from around the globe.

There have been unfortunate political controversies among nations participating in the Olympic Games, and China was involved in a dispute about representation between the Republic of China, or Taiwan, and the People's Republic of China. China contested the representation of two "Chinas," which became a debated issue of face confrontation. The response was the boycotting of the games between 1956 and 1980.

In 1984, China made a comeback at the Los Angeles Summer Olympics to win a total of thirty-two medals. In the 1988 games in Seoul, China won twenty-eight medals. In the 1992 games in Barcelona, China won fifty-four medals. In the 1996 games in Atlanta, China won fifty medals. In the 2000 games in Sydney, China won fifty-eight medals. In the 2004 games in Athens, China won sixty-three medals. Last but not least, China in 2008 dazzled the world by hosting the Olympics in Beijing and won one hundred medals, ranking her the number-one contender of the 2008 Olympic Games. The Chinese people were ecstatic because China had showed the world that she was no longer the "sick man of Asia," as she had been called during the period of the two Sino-Japanese Wars.

The preparations for the 2008 Olympic Games need further discussion because they help us to better understand the business of face in China. To China, hosting the games in Beijing was a matter of national pride, akin to inviting a friend for dinner at home. The host of the dinner in this case was China. At the Beijing airport one could see an eye-catching welcoming banner that read, "It is a joy to have friends from afar." The same message also appeared on the huge electronic board at the opening ceremony to underscore the country's tradition of hospitality because the message is in fact a quote from Confucius's *Analects*.

Let us use the analogy of inviting friends home for dinner. The host makes every effort to ensure the home is presentable and the meal well prepared because anything less is a loss of face. To achieve this goal, the country spent billions to transform or refurbish its infrastructure, transportation, broadband telecommunications, hotels, sports facilities, and even its air quality to support the massive sporting events in Beijing and other sites outside the capital city. China wanted global recognition and internationalization. She wanted face, and she got it in the 2008 Olympic Games.

After a fast review of China's modern history, one starts to see face as an emotional state with two opposing flanks of shame and honor. On the negative side of losing face are defeat, humiliation, incompetence, and low self-esteem. On the positive side of gaining face are power, high self-esteem, an ego boost, recognition, pride, prestige, and looking good. Figure 7.1 shows the yin and yang of the two opposing flanks of the face.

It is an oversimplification to show positive and negative face as stand-alone elements because they are not. The elements in figure 7.1 mimic the yin and yang of Chinese philosophy. In figure 7.1, the outer big circle represents the universe, or everything, while the black and white teardrop shapes inside the circle represent the interaction of the two opposing groups of elements, called yin (black) and yang (white), causing everything to happen. Yin represents the dark elements of negativity; yang represents the bright elements of positivity.

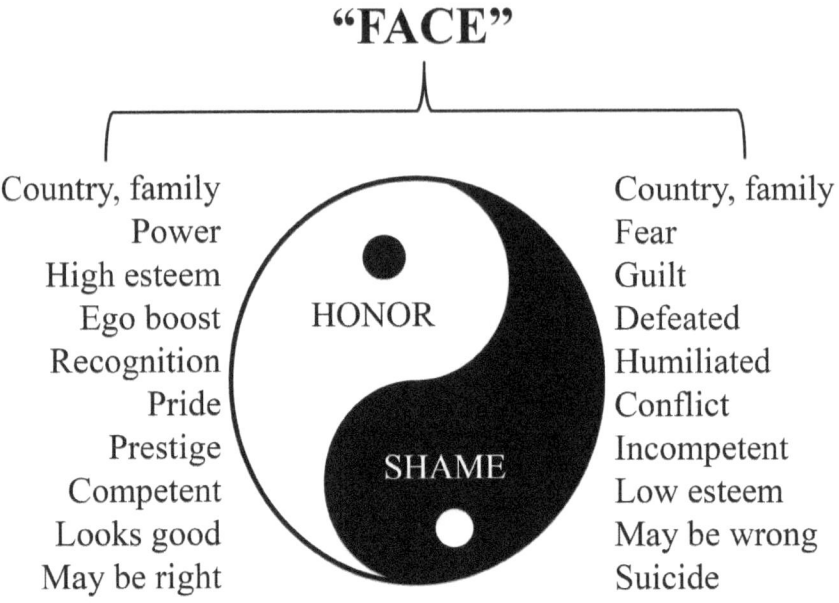

Figure 7.1. The yin and yang of face.

In figure 7.1, embedded inside each teardrop shape is still another small circle of the opposite, yin and yang. The emotional states of honor and shame, like yin and yang, seldom exist independently; they interact with each other in the attempt to achieve equilibrium. Any disequilibrium affects the person involved in an action.

What follows are nine popular Chinese expressions. Nine is a lucky Chinese number connoting longevity. The expressions reflect the importance of the face culture with regard to honor and shame:

1. *All about face*, meaning a change of viewpoint or attitude because of fame and favor: The discussion got heated because the issue is all about face.
2. *Gain face*, meaning a gain in pride: Marilyn's outstanding performance at the concert gained face for her family.
3. *Get one's face back*, meaning to make it up: He invested extra time in the special project to gain his face back from a previous failure.
4. *All of one's face has been lost*, meaning very shameful: All of his face has been lost due to his cheating on the final examination.

5. *Big face*, meaning to have influence and leverage: Despite Johnny's inexperience, he is likely to get the job because of his father's big face.
6. *Red face and white face*, meaning good guy and bad guy.
7. *Break one's fake face*, meaning to expose the truth: She broke her fake face by exposing the real intention behind the attempt.
8. *Face-off*, meaning confrontation: A face-off between the boss and the employee is likely because the boss painted the subordinate into a corner.
9. *Give face to*, meaning to show respect: In a formal Chinese banquet, the guests are considered disrespectful or seen as not giving face to the host if they refuse the dinner invitation.

These expressions are ingrained in the Chinese way of thinking. They reveal the mechanisms behind the Chinese belief system. The dynamics of their use reflect how the cultural disposition works. These expressions about Chinese face provide a better understanding of how and why culture matters. In the case of the 2008 Olympic Games in Beijing, China did everything she could to fight for the top spot in the total medal count because it was all about national pride, and it was undoubtedly a matter of face.

## GAINING FACE WITH THE GROSS DOMESTIC PRODUCT

Olympic medal count, well publicized on worldwide media, is one small facet of China's face gain in recent years; the real substance of the face gain started years before the Beijing Olympics. Yes, you guessed it. It is the gross domestic product (GDP) of China. Why is GDP important?

GDP is a monetary measure of the value of all goods and services produced by a country over a predetermined period—say, a year. Measuring GDP is similar to determining the worth of a person based on all assets, investments, and revenues. GDP is a useful indicator of worth because it allows ready comparison among countries or regions around the globe. The quantitative determination of GDP is complicated, and we will leave it to diligent economists; suffice it to say that China is currently a global economic power second only to the United States. In a few more years, according to some predictions, China might even be the top-ranked economic power by GDP.

Do you know that GDP relates to the skills of the workforce? This is how education is connected in the loop of this chapter's discussion. Let the truth be told that countries like the United States and China must have good schools to succeed economically. Good education, a critical investment in human capital, can be shown in the average years of schooling, which is fine as a broad measure; still, a more pointed question needs to be asked about the content of schooling. What has been learned? Test score data are used to evaluate the quality of the cognitive skills of those entering the workforce (see chapter 6).

Thus far, we have presented a flyover of some two hundred years in modern history to discuss the concept of face in a nation with 1.38 billion people and five thousand years of civilization. The brief history accounts for how a nation can lose or fight for its face. Though intangible and abstract, face is a very important standard for regulating and managing action and inaction. To further understand the Chinese way of thinking, let us leave the national stage for an arena of social entertainment in China.

## USING CONSOLATION AS A CRITICAL SOCIAL SKILL

Losing and gaining face are the two extremes of the face continuum. At these extremes, people can be either depressed or elevated emotionally. To avoid emotional downturn, the parties involved need to manage the situation through consolation, or having a "consoling face."

Let us see how consoling works as a social skill on a popular reality TV show in China. *Super Girl* is one of China's most popular talent shows, similar to *American Idol* in the United States. *Super Girl* was viewed by more than 400 million people in China in 2005, making it one of the most successful shows in Chinese television history.

Why is the show so popular? In essence, it is an out-of-the-culture sensation for the audience because of how participants dress in unorthodox clothing, sing, perform, scream, gyrate wildly on stage, punch their fists into the air, and freely show emotion. In addition, viewers vote by phone or text message for the performers whom they favor. People were wondering if this smacked of democracy, and the government thought this might be too democratic. For this reason the show was controversial; conservatives in the government called it a poison for the youth and demanded sterner control and regulation.

In a typical American TV game show, the judges make brief remarks about the performances, and the votes are counted to declare the winner and loser. China's *Super Girl* contest is interesting in terms of the participants' response to winning and losing. The viewers from outside the Chinese culture will note that a disparate amount of time is spent on emotional face consoling by the performers and the judges, working hard to help protect and save face. Harsh words such as "You are the loser" or "You are out" are seldom used because those are not appropriate to save face for the loser.

## WESTERN FACE VERSUS CHINESE FACE

One can argue that the culture of face is not unique to the Chinese because the West also has a version of "Western face." Western culture tends to pay more attention to the individual as independent and self-reliant. For that reason, in raising a child, the focus is on helping him or her to develop a strong sense of individuality with personal confidence and integrity. A child's poor behavior or performance is often blamed on the individual and attributed to his or her own irresponsibility; therefore, the assertion that a child is not doing well in school is a guilt-based accusation. The Western culture of face is about individualism.

In contrast, Chinese culture has softened the concept of the individual and emphasized the integrity of the family or group, in which the individual is only a part of the whole. If a student is misbehaving or performing poorly in school, it is more the fault of the family and the lack of home education, or *jia jiao* in Chinese, as mentioned in chapter 4. A student not doing well in school is a serious matter of shame for the family because the parents are blamed for not raising the child properly. The assertion that a child is performing poorly is a shame-based accusation of the family and the clan. The Chinese face culture is about collectivism.

## EPISODES OF LOSING FACE

Now that I have laid the broad foundational concept of face, we will turn to three episodes concerning Chinese face in the context of schools and education.

Hong Kong International School (HKIS) is a well-established institution in Hong Kong, China. It is a Christian private school that follows an American-style curriculum, offering various Advanced Placement courses. It has a unique student population of international students representing many countries.

At the beginning of one school term, the student government organized a kickoff celebration and invited both faculty and students to participate. Faculty and students were divided into teams. Members of the teams were well mixed, and just by coincidence one group contained predominantly American faculty.

There followed a series of entertaining games. Everything started out lightheartedly, and each team took turns winning at a variety of friendly competitions. One of the last races required the teams to use chopsticks to carry a raw egg across a finish line. Players had to transfer the egg from one person to the next without touching or dropping it.

During this particular event, the jovial atmosphere of the game changed dramatically due to its extreme challenge. The teams giggled at the idea of the American faculty team even having a chance to win with the chopsticks. The race started, and the American faculty team quickly took the lead by a long stretch. The cheerful laughter subsided, and the teams even stopped cheering. Finally, the runner-up teams struggled for second place in awkward silence.

At the end of the race, some of the students congratulated the American faculty team. Interestingly, none of the Chinese teachers said a word. One Chinese faculty member finally explained that the American faculty team had caused the adults to lose face not just by winning but by defeating them by a wide margin. Another Chinese student expounded that the Americans were not supposed to be good at using chopsticks, simply because that was perceived as an exclusively Chinese skill.

Working with Chinese people often requires a certain level of skill with intercultural communication. The art is to make sure that they do not lose face. The loss of face at the HKIS festivity can be described as a minor embarrassment because it was only a game and could serve as a good transitional conversation piece to stimulate new connections for members of the school community. Now we will study a situation with a more intense level of losing face.

Mr. Zhang, principal of a top-ranked provincial high school, returned to his school office late one evening after a board meeting to find that he had left his set of keys inside the office. He was locked out, and the office assistant was nowhere to be found because it was after hours. Mr. Zhang phoned several times for help, and Mrs. He, the office assistant, did not answer. Mr. Zhang was very upset and all fired up. Losing his calm, he e-mailed Mrs. He and blamed her for leaving the office and just assuming that

Mr. Zhang had his keys. The e-mail went on to say that effective immediately, Mrs. He was not to leave the office without checking with him, including during breaks, at the lunch hour, and at the end of the day. To make the matter worse, he cc'd the other board members just to show that Mrs. He had made a grave mistake.

To Mr. Zhang's surprise, he found an e-mail from the office assistant waiting for him early the next morning. Mrs. He included the original e-mail from Mr. Zhang and defended her actions as unquestionably right. She said that, for security, she had to lock the office door; that was her responsibility. She continued that the mistake lay with Mr. Zhang for not carrying his keys with him to the meeting. At the end of the message, she said that Mr. Zhang had no right to make demands of her private time, including breaks, lunchtimes, and after-work hours. Mrs. He also cc'd the e-mail to all the board members as well as the other assistant school administrators.

By the end of the week the incident had become the talk of the school community. What happened? Why was the exchange between the abusive boss and his defensive subordinate so heated? Do you think that the school community was discussing who was right and who was wrong? Think again. The real issue below the surface was face. Mr. Zhang had made a mistake by cc'ing his reprimand to the board members, which essentially turned a private rebuke into a public disgrace. On the other hand, Mrs. He also erred in cc'ing her rebuttal to the board members and other administrators, publicly humiliating Mr. Zhang in the workplace. At the end of the day, the episode was not about right or wrong; it was about face, about honor, about a Chinese administrative assistant defending herself, which ultimately cost her her job. In the next and final episode, we will look at the ultimate sacrifice after a loss of face.

A middle school student in Hohhot, in the Inner Mongolia autonomous region of China, killed himself by jumping from the top floor of a building after learning that his test score had dropped. A secondary student in Sichuan Province slashed her wrists and took poison after learning that she had done poorly on the college entrance examination; she knew that she would not be admitted to a university with her poor scores. Another primary school girl in Nanking hanged herself at home after she failed to finish her homework. These are among the many reports of student suicides in the news in China. What was at issue, and why did the students kill themselves?

The reports reveal that the suicides occurred frequently when students were under stress related to losing face. It is a no-brainer that students in

China are under high pressure—from parents, teachers, and peers—to do well in school. Failure to do so brings more than just shame. It is a humiliation and public loss of face. Many people believe that students, at their tender age, need more communication from the parents and teachers. Unfortunately, parents and teachers are also under pressure to help the students to do well. It is an ill-fated vicious cycle of losing face for everybody, and finding the solution to the deep-rooted problem remains a challenge.

*Chapter Eight*

# Connections

"You cannot clap with one hand."

### EAST IS EAST, AND WEST IS WEST

An American visiting professor gave a university class in China the word set *bamboo*, *lion*, and *panda*. He asked the students to select the two most closely related words, with the understanding that there was no right or wrong answer. The students gave two sets of selections. The first was *lion* and *panda*. The second and largest was *bamboo* and *panda*. When asked about their reasoning, the first group explained that lions and pandas both belong to the animal group. The second group explained that, as pandas eat bamboo, the relation refers to the animal and what it eats.

The professor repeated the exercise back in the United States in Illinois after his teaching assignment in China. The American students made the same two major selections. This time, however, the majority of students selected *lion* and *panda*, with the next largest selection being *bamboo* and *panda*. Both student groups offered similar rationales for their choices.

The results of the word set exercise are thought-provoking because—assuming that selection is a willed human behavior stemming from the mind—the preferences of the Chinese and the American students apparently differ. The simple exercise points to the possible impact of socialization on the way people think and act.

The decision to group *lion* with *panda* is taxonomic: both belong to the animal group. Categories populated by nouns such as *lion* and *panda* imply little to no relationship between the words. The two animals are not even in the same food chain ecologically. On the other hand, putting *panda* and *bamboo* in the same group states a relationship because pandas eat bamboo. The verb *eat* describes the relationship between the animal and its food.

What is the predominant Chinese mind-set for making connections? The Chinese language has no clear noun distinction to indicate "a panda," "pandas," "the pandas," and "the panda." Only context cues us to the difference between "Many pandas are sleeping in the bamboo forest" and "The panda is the national treasure of the Chinese people." Interestingly, the generic category generally gets used less frequently in the Chinese language.

Let us study a second example and listen to how two hostesses ask customers whether they would like drink refills in a downtown tea shop. Is it possible that the Chinese and American ways of thinking differ? A Chinese hostess asks, "Drink more?" An American hostess asks, "More tea?" What is the difference? The Chinese hostess speaks more behaviorally because the beverage is clear from the context; therefore the verb *drink* is more relevant. For the American hostess, subject matter is more relevant because the acts of drinking and refilling the cup are assumed. In Eastern traditions, objects, including humans, that do not interact with the environment are not important and of no concern. However, when objects interact with the environment to yield a behavioral relationship, people need to take note to ensure a proper response. In essence, the object by itself is not as important as the connections that it generates with the environment.

Let us look at a third example, this time a newspaper report, to see if Chinese and Western reporting or journalism differs. "On Friday, November 15, 1991, a former postal clerk walked into a regional postal office and opened fire with a sawed-off 0.22-caliber rifle, killing three workers and wounding six, before fatally wounding himself, the authorities said" (Levin 1991). The report goes on to describe the postal clerk as mentally unstable, with a short fuse and a history of repeatedly threatening violence. The descriptions tend to focus on the perpetrator's personal traits and past behavior. *World Journal*, a Chinese-language newspaper, describes the incident differently. Its account notes that the postal clerk saw his supervisor as the enemy; he was being fired, and the gun was available to him. This report tends to focus the situation, which involved a complex relationship.

The triangulation of these three examples confirms the hypothesis that the general Chinese and Western ways of thinking and doing business differ. East is East, and West is West. The Chinese look at things and their situational connections. The idiom "You cannot clap with one hand" at the beginning of the chapter points to the fact that clapping involves two hands and thus involves a relationship.

In the business of education in China, connection is everything. That means parents must connect with children or students at home to guide them down the path of achievement. In turn, students must connect with teachers before teachers can connect them to the learning materials. The web of connections widens and gets more complicated as we move from family to school to community. In this chapter, the discussion relates only to human connections to enhance the impact of intercultural communication in education.

Many years ago, when China opened up to the world, Western professionals, such as researchers, teachers, students, experts, businesspeople, and consultants, flocked to the Middle Kingdom only to find themselves in the midst of a totally different culture. It was logical to think that language was the front-and-center barrier, so they came with their pocket language translators and uttered some sentences in Mandarin. That helped until they hit another roadblock: the culture of connections and face. Thus, the steep challenge of interpersonal communication remained.

Proper interpersonal communication with Chinese people depends on harmonious group connections. To attain harmony, all parties must act according to their specific position in a group hierarchy. For instance, if you are the school principal, you play the role of a supervisor; if you are the office assistant, you play the role of a subordinate. Dissonance arises when members of the communication group step out of their roles. How realistic is this goal of harmony? Let us look further into Confucianism.

Harmony, according to Confucius, is the philosophical coexistence of people and the environment in nonconflicting relationships. In theory, the practice of love and adherence to social norms are the foundations of good human relationships. Confucius further explained that the perfect man harmonizes, but he does not necessarily seek sameness; the petty person narrowly seeks sameness but does not harmonize. For Confucius, a levelheaded person respects different ideas and works with different people without following them mindlessly. Isn't this like saying that good human relationships respect differences and encourage reason and openness?

Making the right connections circumvents red tape and helps all parties arrive at the final destination—success. Education is about people and is not excused from the golden rule of making good human connections. In figure

8.1, the right-hand side illustrates a Western connection web; the left-hand side represents the intense connection web of the East. Please note that some connections are direct, like family members; others are indirect, like friends. In human relationships, blood is thicker than water with few exceptions. Do not get confused when the younger generations in China call old-timers "uncle" and "aunt." Such forms of address show respect and do not necessarily indicate a blood relationship.

The remainder of the chapter discusses relationship etiquette related to fostering connections.

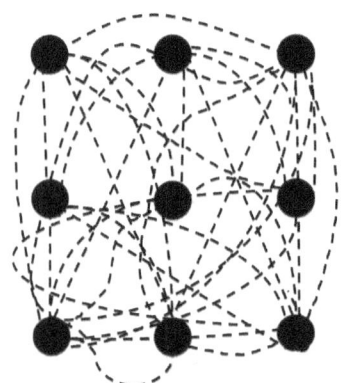 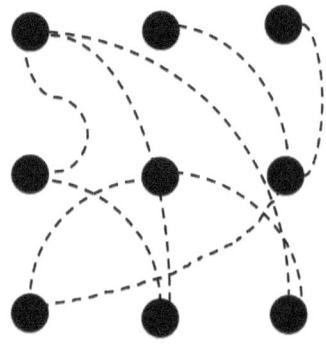

**Figure 8.1. Connections.**

## THE ETIQUETTE OF IMPRESSIONS AND CONNECTIONS

A student meets with a teacher to discuss classwork; a teacher consults with a supervisor about school retention strategies; parents discuss a student's report card with a teacher: Education is undoubtedly a people business. Proper people business, even in education, requires that individuals know and practice common etiquette that will help them to relax, avoid embarrassment, and focus on the matter at hand.

The following business etiquette is valuable for making good impressions and connections:

- Handshakes
- Introductions
- Exchanging business cards
- Name dropping

- Speaking the language
- Meeting protocol
- Dining protocol
- Gift exchanges
- Dressing for success

Business in China relies heavily on personal connections: Make sure you have some. Do you know someone who has the authority to make big decisions? That is a relationship. It is crucial to establish good connections with key contacts regardless of the business that you conduct. Attending networking events, contacting professional associations, and following up on personal introductions are all good ways to start the relationship-building process.

An American teacher with extensive qualifications applied many summers ago to teach in an international school in China. The teacher did not hear back from the school; probably there were already tons of similar applications on the principal's desk. By chance, the international school principal came over to America for a business visit and met the teacher at a conference. The next summer, the teacher applied to the same school and received a summer appointment in a matter of weeks. The successful teacher had gone beyond the previous paper application with connections.

Remember the last time that you met with a school official? Do you recall some of the introductory gestures that you both made? Business meetings start with handshakes, introductions, and business card exchanges.

Remember not to be aggressive with the handshake. Do not worry if you get a limp initial handshake. When the meeting goes well, you may be on the receiving end of a prolonged firm handshake. In Western business meetings, people may find themselves in a handshake contest to see who has the firmer grip, especially among men. In China, the question is who will let go first. Do not feel uncomfortable about the continued shake if your counterpart enjoys it—it is a compliment.

Chinese value rank and position, and this is by no means a gesture to build fences. You need to know whom to talk to and vice versa so that the communication can be meaningful and purposeful. It is important to address your counterparts by their titles, such as *principal*, *director*, and *chair*. If a person has a PhD, address him or her as *doctor* or *professor*, and so on. Know who the high-ranking person in the room is and address him or her first. Addressing the second-in-command first in a meeting will be an insult to the top boss.

Speak your name clearly and remember to state both the institution you represent and your position. Interestingly, Chinese may state the institution first, the work title second, and then their name last when introducing themselves to others. Chinese people follow an orderly group categorization; in this case the institution is more important than the individual. Introducing the cogs before the wheel can be seen as Westernized or, more specifically, Americanized.

Most likely a school officer will give you a business card in both hands, and you should do the same in return. Please remember that using both hands is a sign of respect, and respect builds relationships. Remember that this is your first chance to make an impression. Immediately putting away the card would be a careless mistake. Instead, you should read it carefully to understand and recognize the person's position in the organization before putting it respectfully into your pocket. The card gives you important clues. The title is important because this is how your hosts decide who should be invited to meetings or to dinner, what weight your words carry, and where to seat you.

Would you expect an office assistant to give you credible information about the school budget? Certainly not. She may have the information but not be in the right hierarchical position to share it. This is why business card exchange is a standard procedure when meeting people for the first time. The card announces the person's organization and position in it. That information can help you determine appropriately what questions to ask and what information to share.

Good relations take time to build from the ground up, and sometimes there are shortcuts. A father might come to a prestigious school looking to enroll his child. All things being equal, he might find the wait to see the school director short if he says, "I am the brother-in-law of the school's director," assuming that is indeed the case. It is all about instant connection and name dropping.

How can two people build relationships if they cannot communicate in the same language? Make sure a visitor knows the language capabilities of the host or vice versa before a meeting. Some Westerners may start speaking in their native language even if the Chinese listener has limited understanding of it. It would be better for a person to bring his own interpreter if the other person has little or no English capability. As a Westerner, try your best to speak a little or even a few words in Chinese. This shows that you are eager to make the connection.

Have Chinese-language brochures or presentation materials about your institution to share with your hosts. While your contact in the institution may speak perfect English, the higher-up decision-makers may not. It will be a challenge for a presenter not equipped with materials in the appropriate language to convince the audience. Many people in China have better ability to understand English in printed materials than to speak it.

Meetings, especially with government officials, may follow a formal protocol. The leader of the hosting party is likely to introduce himself and his team and then to state his views on the matter in question or discussion. The leader of your party should follow the same meeting protocol. Subordinate members of the Chinese party will not usually speak unless asked to do so; doing the same allows the Chinese party to see who is in charge and who on your own team may have expertise in a given area.

Remember not to sit down when you enter a conference room. Seating will be designated by rank and position. Normally, the center seat facing the door is for the very important person (VIP). Be patient and wait until you are told where to sit.

Dining is often a way of doing business because the activity allows the host to show hospitality. The dining experience also allows people to cultivate friendships and strengthen connections. As in business meetings, the hosts determine the food and seating. Let us touch on eating and toasting customs next.

Follow your hosts' cues. Start eating only when your hosts begin. There will be cold dishes, such as peanuts and pickled vegetables, on the dining table when you are seated; wait to be invited before you dig in. At formal dinners, serving staff may keep up a steady rotation of dishes. The server may frequently give you a clean plate—not to give the dishwasher more work but to give the diner the distinct taste of the individualized food flavors. The predictable order of the dish parade is nonmeat appetizers, followed by various choices of meat, and then a fish dish. In the north, the fish dish is heavy with sauce; in the south, the fish is usually steamed to the right texture with ginger and scallion. The end portion of the food parade would include a staple, usually rice, noodles, or dumplings, and finish with a dessert or fresh-cut fruit medley.

Chinese believe that eating is a soothing and sharing experience that brings people together for business, celebration, and even consolation. Chinese will offer you plenty of food. It is polite to accept and sample food even if you have dietary restrictions. How do you reject unwanted food that is already on your plate? A nod to the serving staff for a clean plate will allow you to get rid of food that you do not want inconspicuously. In contrast, cleaning your plate may be perceived as a sign that you are enjoying the food and want more.

Chinese eating utensils are highly multipurpose because chopsticks are used for practically everything except soup and sauce. It is okay to ask for a fork and knife if you find that you keep dropping food with chopsticks. Westerners are accustomed to dining with serving utensils, but serving utensils are often not used with family, which is a possible occasion to make or break a connection. It is easy to understand the custom when a husband shares the same hamburger and soda with his wife because they are family. Boyfriends and girlfriends might do the same just to show that they are close and connected.

Alcoholic beverages, such as beer and wine, can be preferred at banquets, especially among men. There may be many toasts during a meal. Follow the leader. Let the hosts initiate the toasts, and you can toast them in return. Do not drink from the toasting glass except during a toast, and do not let the size of the glass fool you because the contents can knock you out. Let the hosts know if you have medical or personal reasons for not drinking; both are acceptable. You should advise your host at the beginning of the banquet or even beforehand to avoid unnecessary embarrassment. To avoid overdrinking, take a light sip every time you are offered a toast drink. A typical toast gesture is for two people to raise and touch glasses. If the person who offers you the toast is on the opposite side of the table, you still can raise your glass, but do not reach across the table to touch glasses. Instead tap the bottom of your drinking glass several times on the table right in front of you. Three taps are the custom, as three is a lucky number in China.

Drinking is seen as a show of friendship, when partners can let their hair down a little to make connections. If the people at a banquet are very comfortable with each other, it is common to go around toasting individuals at the party. Take your lead from your hosts, and you will be safe.

Meals are generally social events in a business context. Conversations around the table are likely to be chitchat not about business. Although the focus of the sociability may not be the food per se, there will be pride in the offerings provided.

Who pays the bill? The host pays. Do not display money or a credit card; it is not polite. If you are the host, take care of the bill out of the view of your guests. Have someone slip out and settle the tab. Waiting until your guests have left before paying is acceptable. In the case of informal get-togethers, like happy hours, the unwritten rule is that the person who has done the inviting or who is in the management position pays. Or maybe he pays this time and you pay next time. Unlike in the West, bill sharing is not common unless by previous mutual agreement.

When going for meals, Chinese friends may "fight" for the bill at the end. This is an amusing Chinese cultural practice that one needs to understand to avoid needless confusion and embarrassment because the fight can range from a harmless scuffle to a more assertive wrestle. Frequently a face thing drives the bill-grabbers to press for picking up the tab. As described in chapter 1, money is a symbol of success in the traditional Chinese way of thinking. For that reason, the "fighter" impresses that he can afford to spend money, or in this case pay the check. All in all, the person who finally gets the bill has shown off his elite status and come across as looking good. How do you react to such a fight for the bill? Sit back or join in for the fine cultural experience, but be prepared to pay.

Professionals dress for success, and this holds true also in China. Government officials and top management dress formally for meetings, while other professionals may wear something other than a suit and tie. If you are not sure, go formal—it will convey respect and professionalism. In the summertime, men may go casual, but shorts are never appropriate.

An American professor received a distinctive invitation to conduct special summer faculty training in China. He was fully attired and found upon arrival that the campus buildings were not air-conditioned. He persevered in wearing suits and ties until the end of the summer assignment. The following summer he was invited back for another round of faculty training. He replaced the shirts and ties with polo shirts but still kept a summer-weight Bahamas blazer. The attire was still heavy because summertime in some parts of China can be steamy. Lo and behold, the professor returned three more summers to the same university and eventually learned that short-sleeved polo shirts and dress khaki pants are acceptable and still respectable. The moral of the story is that it took the professor five summers to adjust to the dress code and make the dress connections.

Gifts are usually exchanged at the end of an introductory meeting or at a banquet. Gift-giving is a widespread Chinese custom that visitors should prepare for, especially on a first visit. The following are some easy-to-follow dos and don'ts.

On a group visit, a single group gift is presented to the leader of the Chinese organization. Gifts should be presented from the leader of the visiting group to the leader of the Chinese group and vice versa. Gifts should not be too expensive and may carry the identity of your affiliated organization or institution. A flag or plaque with the crest or logo of the organization carries real meaning and therefore brings pride to the giver. Chinese love red and gold, which represent prosperity and are also the colors of the national insignia. Avoid black, white, and blue; these are colors for funerals. Remember always to give and receive gifts with two hands. It is similar to the two-hand protocol for exchanging business cards. Be aware that the recipient may initially refuse the gift politely. The giver needs to persevere, and in the end, the recipient will accept.

Avoid giving scissors and clocks. Scissors and other sharp objects, such as knives or letter openers, are cutting instruments, and they are bad for building or reinforcing relationships. The Chinese words for "giving clocks" sound like "paying funeral respect." The gift of a clock could be misinterpreted as an end to the partnership, as in a funeral. Look at the gift, and compliment it suitably as a sign of admiration and appreciation.

## SOME WORDS OF ADVICE

The ability to get along is universally cherished anywhere in the world. In China, achieving interpersonal harmonized connection is the crucial measure of one's competence in social interaction to avoid confrontations. People follow the described etiquettes of impression and connections when they meet and interact. Are their actions coming from the heart? If yes, the feelings are sincere and genuine. Anything not coming from the heart is superficial and could just cover possible conflicts under the surface. Genuine harmony in the real world is difficult to achieve, and therefore many people settle for surface relationships as social performance. People from the Western world often get confused by the preference for superficial relationships and even see them as challenging to their integrity. What follows are the four principles to make and maintain harmonious connections:

- *Save face for others.* Chinese place tremendous significance on face and social interactions. Therefore, one important way to maintain harmonious relationships among people is to respect the needs of others and to always give them face. If you make someone lose face, you will lose the respect

not only of the person you have wronged but also of others who are aware of the wrongdoing. Making face for superiors is regarded as polite and sometimes necessary. Steer away from open disagreement, conflict, and competition, and replace negativities with mutual understanding and tolerance.
- *Practice mutuality.* Reciprocate a favor with a favor. In Chinese social interaction, doing a favor for someone in need or repaying someone who has provided help on previous occasions is the communicative principle of *renqing*. In a way, one who receives a favor is in debt to the person doing it. It is a common social standard for people to get along by building interdependency and mutual respect. It is difficult for Westerners to recognize the hidden responsibility when done a favor or given a gift. In Chinese contexts, if you cannot return a favor at a convenient time, apologize and promise seriously to do it someday in the future.
- *Be moderate.* Moderation is another element needed to achieve balanced relationships. To be moderate in one's behavior is a major principle of the *Doctrine of the Mean* in Confucianism, and it signifies having achieved a balance. So how do people achieve the goal of being moderate in social behavior? Subdue raw emotion in public to reduce personal desires and promote the welfare of the group. Even strong feelings should be expressed in a moderate manner. Chinese people commonly express negative emotions in a contained, reserved, indirect, and implicit fashion. For example, students seldom question their teachers in class; however, they may express their opinions freely after the class is over. And Chinese businesspeople seldom take aggressive measures to press for what they want in negotiations. Instead, they are likely to use win-win strategies to maintain joint relationships.
- *Always think about what is good for the group.* In social interactions, many people draw serious distinctions between insiders and outsiders to regulate the important process of decision-making. Within a group the force of cohesion is always strong, and mutual compromise is a key to positive connections. When speaking on behalf of the group, a person often prefaces his ideas by saying, "In our opinion" or "We think" instead of "In my opinion" or "I think" to reinforce the harmony of the group. Examples of groups are family, school, and company. "One tree does not make a forest" and "A single flower does not make a spring" are two Chinese idioms that summarize the importance of the group and the individual's hierarchical position and role within it. Figure 8.2 summarizes the

critical elements of building relationships together. The size of the overlap area correlates to the strength of the relationships, although the contribution from the individual elements might not be the same.

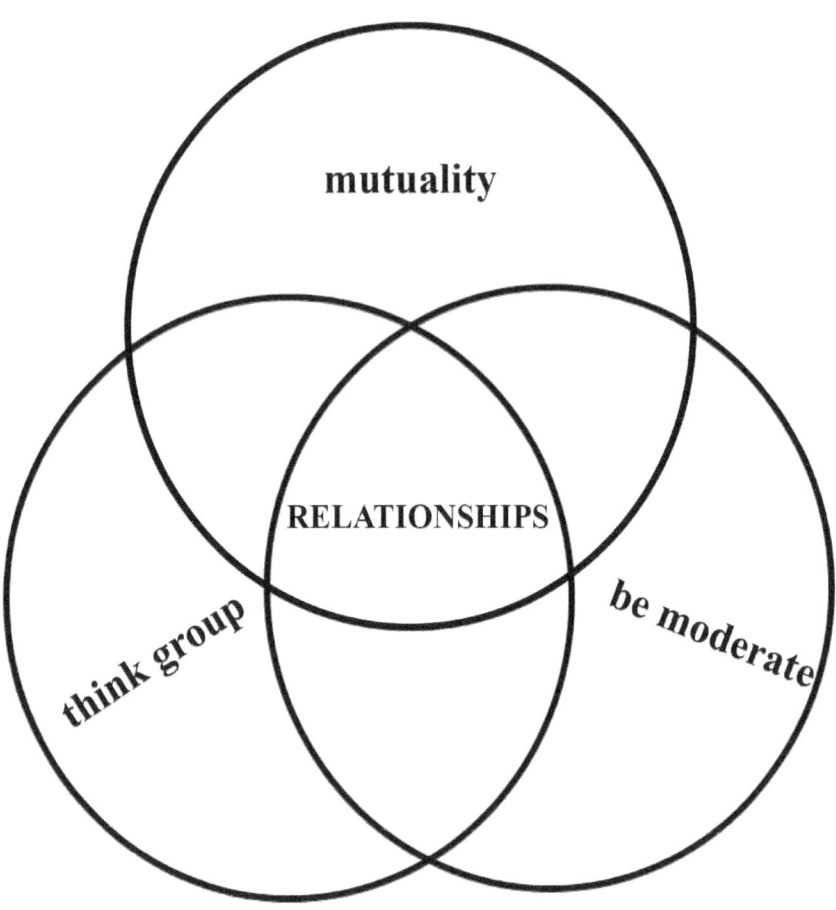

Figure 8.2.  Elements of relationships.

# Afterword

Education is a system of teaching and learning over time. The critical elements of the system are the information, the processes, and most importantly the values and beliefs being delivered via another complex system of language communication. These elements form and sustain what people believe to be important and over a long period become the building blocks of an advanced stage of human society we call civilization.

People wonder why Chinese civilization has managed to endure for thousands of years despite so many dynastic changes in its history. A part of the answer is its deep-rooted educational system, which goes beyond the advancement of information to preserve and stabilize the Confucian philosophy of harmony.

Go back in history, and see how the Han Chinese, with their well-established civilization based on a well-oiled educational system, assimilated the Mongols between the Song and Ming Dynasties. In a recent press conference, President Xi Jinping was asked whether China will ever be a nation of aggressors. He answered the question diplomatically by asking whether China was ever an aggressor in major world conflicts. The philosophy of Confucian harmony endures.

When education is such a critical building block of human civilization, what would have happened in its absence? The answer is disaster. In 1966 and 1967, the world witnessed the dark side of China during the Cultural Revolution. For ten years the educational system failed, the minds of the people came to a standstill, and the nation crumbled. Even today, descendants from that dark era still feel the void left by a total lack of formal learning and the steering of the belief system of the entire nation in a completely different direction.

China is currently the most populous nation on earth and relies on a highly competitive educational system to regulate the minds of citizens. Through meritocracy, people are selected to collectively support the ultimate Chinese dream of becoming the next world power.

The system of education is rendered even more convoluted when teaching, learning, and testing are grounded in the subtle culture of face (*lian*) and relationships (*guanxi*). Education in China is multifarious, and to explain it using eight concepts—*success, meritocracy, parents, schooling, cram schools, examinations, face,* and *connections*—is undoubtedly a challenging undertaking.

Around the world, academic achievement is a good way to attain personal success. Chinese students are no different in aggressively striving for top performance in high-stakes examinations to the point that the thrill of learning is tainted by the bore of test-taking. Zhuang Zi shows us the distinction between the enjoyment of performing a task versus the boredom of doing it for a less-than-enjoyable purpose. He says,

> When an *archer* is *shooting* for *nothing*, he has all his skills. If he *shoots* for a *brass buckle*, he is already nervous. If he shoots for *a prize of gold*, he goes blind or see two *targets*. His skills have not changed, but the *prize* divides him. He cares. He thinks more of *winning* than of *shooting*, and his need to *win* drains him of power.

Let us recompose the above and replace some of the words in italics to reflect what Chinese students are really up against in Chinese education today:

> When a *student* is *learning* for *no specific purpose*, he has all his skills. If he *learns* for a *test*, he is already nervous. If he *learns* for *the gaokao*, he goes blind or sees two *goals*. His skills have not changed, but *the gaokao* divides him. He cares. He thinks more of *passing the gaokao* than of *learning*, and his need to *pass the gaokao* drains him of power.

# Appendix

## A Chronology of China

| Period/Dynasty/Country | Date | Reference |
|---|---|---|
| Period of the Five Imperial Rulers | 3000–2070 BC | |
| Xia Dynasty | 2070–1600 BC | |
| Shang Dynasty | 1600–1046 BC | |
| Zhou Dynasty | 1046–256 BC | Confucius, Sun Tzu, Qu Yuan, Warring States Period |
| Qin Dynasty | 221–207 BC | |
| Han Dynasty | 202 BC–AD 220 | Kong Rong |
| Three Kingdoms Period | AD 220–280 | Zhuge Liang, Cao Cao |
| Western Jin Dynasty | AD 265–316 | |
| Eastern Jin Dynasty | AD 317–420 | Mencius |
| Northern and Southern Dynasties | AD 420–589 | |
| Sui Dynasty | AD 581–618 | Imperial examination system |
| Tang Dynasty | AD 618–907 | Du Mu |
| Five Dynasties | AD 907–960 | |
| Song Dynasty | AD 960–1276 | Yue Fei, Wen Tianxiang, Four Books and Five Classics |
| Liao Dynasty | AD 907–1125 | |
| Jin Dynasty | AD 1115–1234 | |
| Yuan Dynasty | AD 1271–1368 | |
| Ming Dynasty | AD 1368–1644 | Zheng Cheng Gong, Zheng He |
| Qing Dynasty | AD 1636–1911 | Qianlong, Lin Zexu |

| | | |
|---|---|---|
| Republic of China | AD 1911–1949 | |
| People's Republic of China | AD 1949 | Mao Zedong |

# References

Beijing Tianli Examination Information Network. (2015). *Entrance Examination Provinces and Cities Nationwide Compilation Full Solution*. Beijing: Tibet People's Publishing House.

Bradsher, K. (2013). In China, Betting It All on a Child in College. *New York Times*, February 17. Retrieved from http://libweb.ben.edu/login?url=http://search.proquest.com/docview/1288152288?accountid=40667.

Gagliardi, G. (2003). *The Art of War: Plus the Ancient Chinese Revealed*. Seattle, WA: Clearbridge Publishing.

Halsall, P. (1997). Qian Long: Letter to King George III, 1793. *Modern History Sourcebook*. Retrieved from http://sourcebooks.fordham.edu/mod/1793qianlong.asp.

Harvard University. (2016). Graduate Speaker Jiang He | Harvard Commencement 2016. Uploaded to YouTube on May 26, 2016. Retrieved on August 26, 2016, from https://www.youtube.com/watch?v=BM2HMoK5aIU.

Larmer B. (2015). *China's Cram Schools*. Upfront.scholastic.com.

Levin, D. P. (1991). Ex-Postal Worker Kills 3 and Wounds 6 in Michigan. *New York Times*, November 15. Retrieved from http://libweb.ben.edu/login?url=http://search.proquest.com/docview/428286444?accountid=40667.

Liyao, L. (2013). Maotanchang: A Town Living on Gaokao. China.org.cn, October 3. Retrieved August 26, 2016, from http://www.china.org.cn/china/2013-10/03/content_30175844.htm.

Thomas Jefferson Foundation, Inc. (n.d.). A Bill for the More General Diffusion of Knowledge. Monticello.org. Retrieved from https://www.monticello.org/site/jefferson/bill-more-general-diffusion-knowledge.

Tian Li National Gaokao Exam Questions Research Center. (2015). *Analysis of the 2014 Gaokao Examination Questions*. Lhaso: Tibet People's Press.

Yang, K. (2013). In China, It's the Grandparents Who "Lean In." *Atlantic*, September 30. Retrieved August 26, 2016, from http://www.theatlantic.com/china/archive/2013/09/in-china-its-the-grandparents-who-lean-in/280097.

# About the Author

**Ovid Wong** is associate science education professor at Benedictine University in Lisle, Illinois, with a joint teaching appointment in the College of Science and the School of Education. He is also a visiting professor of faculty development at Dalian Nationalities University in China. He received his BSc and DipEd from the University of Alberta, his MEd from the University of Washington, and his PhD in curriculum and instruction from the University of Illinois. His experience in public education spans more than twenty years, from inner-city classrooms of Chicago to the suburban office of the assistant school superintendent. In 1989, Dr. Wong received the National Science Foundation's Outstanding Science Teacher in Illinois Award and the National Science Teaching Achievement Recognition (STAR) Award from the National Science Teacher Association. In the same year, he visited the former Soviet Union as the environmental science delegation leader with the Student Ambassador Program. He was the first recipient of the outstanding alumni award from the University of Alberta in 1992 and the first recipient of the distinguished alumni award from the College of Education at the University of Illinois in 1995. In 2013, he received the Distinguished Faculty Award in recognition of his significant achievements in research at Benedictine University. He is author of thirty-three books and received the Midwest Book Author Award from the Children's Reading Roundtable of Chicago. His recent books are dedicated to coaching teachers and students to effectively prepare for state-mandated examinations across the nation with specific editions in Illinois, Michigan, New York, and Ohio.

www.ingramcontent.com/pod-product-compliance
Lightning Source LLC
Chambersburg PA
CBHW020749230426
43665CB00009B/545